In praise of *Befriending Conflict*

Joe Goodbread's *Befriending Conflict* gives substance to the ideal of win-win conflict resolution. His book offers simple, understandable, and practical tools for turning everyday conflicts into opportunities for personal growth and better relationships. and for realizing deep democracy in daily life.

—Arnold Mindell Ph.D.

Author of *Processmind*

Befriending Conflict is an inspiration. Goodbread's easy style, engaging stories and simple "inner work" steps make me feel encouraged and excited to wade into the waters of difficult conversations. *Befriending Conflict* weaves together profound insights with simple conflict resolution steps through fun and easy to read stories. It is ideal for both the seasoned conflict resolution professional and those wanting to bring more honesty and depth to their relationship life.

—Julie Diamond Ph.D.

Vice President of Academic Affairs, Process Work Institute

Befriending Conflict is par excellence amongst resources in field of Conflict Resolution. This book speaks to everyone from the lay person to the corporate executive leader. Engaging with *Befriending Conflict* and working through the many experiential and inner exercises based on a Process Work methodology will transform the way you think about and work with conflict from the inside out. This book will help anyone who struggles with conflict in their life. Opening this book is a doorway to a deep journey that will transform you and those you interact with.

—Cathy Bernatt

Outward Bound International Global Facilitation Network Leader

Books by Joseph Goodbread

Living on the Edge: The mythical, spiritual, and philosophical roots of social marginality

The Dreambody Toolkit: A practical introduction to the philosophy, goals, and practice of process-oriented psychology

Radical Intercourse: How dreams unite us in love, conflict, and other inevitable relationships

BEFRIENDING CONFLICT

EAN-13 9781452856766
LCNN 2010907023

JOE GOODBREAD, PH.D.

BEFRIENDING CONFLICT

HOW TO MAKE CONFLICT SAFER, MORE PRODUCTIVE, AND MORE FUN

PROCESS ORIENTED PSYCHOLOGY PUBLICATIONS

PREFACE

Befriending conflict – what an idea! It came from a project proposed to me by Tim Spalding at a conference in Greece in 2002. The concept was simple: help those who worked in the counties on both sides of the border to Northern Ireland find resources to cope with the tension that permeated the region. Although on the brink of a political settlement, the age-old tensions still persisted. How to help people cope with fear, confusion, and other disturbing states of mind that were a daily feature of their work and lives? We were in Greece for a "Worldwork" seminar – one of a series of ten-day-long workshops held every two years to experiment with an approach to conflict and group dynamics formulated by Arnold Mindell and his colleagues. Tim saw the potential for applying Worldwork concepts to the situations faced daily by himself and his colleagues. And so, the Befriending Conflict project was born.

Befriending Conflict was presented in four 2-day modules spread out over September 2003 to June 2004. The first of these was on "inner work," an approach to dealing with the clouded states of mind that make conflict scary before we every meet our opponents. This book is based on this first module, which was taught by Brid Commins, Kate Jobe, and myself. Kate and I have subsequently refined the original material, presenting it at seminars in Portland, Oregon, Dublin, Ireland, and Warsaw, Poland.

This book is intended as the first in a series. It gives the basic ideas and methods of preparing for conflict using inner work methods. It also gives a taste of how these methods can be applied in real-life situations. Subsequent volumes planned for this series include using these methods in relationship conflicts as well as in specific areas such as legal practice, labor relations, customer relations – in short, any area where conflict can arise. My goal is to provide you with reliable methods for mining conflict's rich potential for deepening relationships and providing unexpected solutions to persistent, thorny problems. I offer this alternative to the more usual tendency to avoid conflict, because conflict that is suppressed has a nasty way of surfacing, unbidden, when it is least welcome. I look forward to your comments, as well as suggestions for further areas of application – particularly those where you think that these methods can never work!

Joe Goodbread
Portland, Oregon
Feb. 5, 2010

ACKNOWLEDGEMENTS

This book was born in September 2003 in Monaghan, Ireland when my partner Kate Jobe and I presented the first module of a cycle of seminars called Befriending Conflict. We owe a tremendous debt to Tim Spalding, then of the Donegal Community Workers Cooperative, and Nora Newell, of the Donegal Women's Center, for conceptualizing and parenting this year-long course.

Our friends and colleagues Brid Commins, Sonja Straub, Jan Dworkin, Robert King, and Reini Hauser all participated in the planning and presentation of the year-long cycle of seminars. Without their creativity and inspiration, this work would never have come into being.

Much of the material in this book is based on the work of Arnold Mindell – teacher, colleague and friend. His pioneering development of the worldwork and deep democracy paradigms inform nearly everything in this book. Although I have cited many details from his work, we have worked so closely over the years that it is hard to say where his ideas leave off and mine begin.

Thanks to friends and colleagues who read early versions of this work – Tony Carlin, Kevin Fahey, Mahir

Sayir, Klaus Haeusler, Juerg Dual, David Bedrick, among others – and contributed valuable comments.

Margaret Ryan did her editorial magic, guiding me to transform the prima materia of my first outpourings into what you see here. Needless to say, any errors are all my own.

Special thanks to Kate Jobe for more than two decades of close collaboration, out of which many of the concepts and exercises were born. She has also been my partner in crime through many of the tales of conflict that add spice to this work. In all of these stories, "I", which I use for the sake of simplicity, really means "We".

Thanks to Sonja Straub for her groudbreaking dissertation on inner criticism, as well as for helping me understand that realizing that I am talking to myself is more than half the job of coming to terms with inner voices.

And thanks above all to my students in Portland, Ireland, and many other places in the world who have helped me with all facets of this work – some by tolerating my attempts to teach it, others by daring to transcend the role structure of student and teacher and engage me in conflict that I hope was as useful to them as it was to me.

CONTENTS

A TALE OF TWO CONFLICTS

It's early morning in New York City. We're in a hotel in midtown Manhattan, and my partner Kate and I are exhausted. We've come from Zurich to teach a seminar on conflict resolution.

We arrived in town two nights ago, thinking we had a hotel reservation, only to discover that our room had been given away to someone else. The best the staff could come up with was a "secondary" room in the back of a large luxury hotel…which meant both of us sleeping in a single bed that reeked of unwashed bodies, alcohol, and cigarettes.

And here we are, comfortable at last in a good room in another hotel…when, at 2 A.M., just as we are getting ready for bed, the toilet overflows. Not just a little water spilling gently over the rim, but a virtual tsunami rises from the bowl, floods the tiny bathroom, jumps the threshold, and saturates the bedroom rug. This is the last straw. The manager eventually finds us another room. By now it is well past 3 A.M., and we have to start work in a few hours.

Checking out the following morning, I can barely contain my rage. I demand that they reduce the price of the room. The desk clerk mumbles a half apology – "I'm sorry you feel that way, Sir," which only feeds my anger. I demand to see a manager...the manager is unavailable. My face is turning purple. Kate later said she was afraid I was going to have a heart attack or become violent. I reach across the desk and grab the credit card slip the clerk has just run and tear it up, then storm out of the lobby.

A hollow victory

I got what I wanted, but it was a hollow victory that left me in a terrible mood for the rest of the morning. I felt that I had polluted the environment with my rage, leaving many people, including myself, worse off than when I started, all for the sake of a few dollars and my injured pride. Add to that the irony that we'd come to New York to teach conflict resolution!

There had to be a better way of handling the situation, a way that would leave the world better off than when the problem started. But I was damned if I knew how to do it.

This episode became the object of an ongoing meditation in the following months and years. I felt sincerely that I had been abused by the hotels with which we dealt. They clearly had more business than they could handle, so my satisfaction was not important to the people who dealt with me. On the other hand, I had to admit to myself that I loved the opportunity to "let it rip," to get furious and see others cringe before my threatening rage. It was only afterwards, when the momentary surge of exhilaration was replaced by a sense of loss, that I regretted what I had done. It was almost like a drug high that left a real "downer" in its wake.

It became clear to me why I got so high on conflict. I grew up as somewhat of an outcast, interested in science and reading at a time when geek was definitely not chic. Afflicted by vision problems that left me without much depth perception and therefore inept at sports, I preferred to do science projects or catch insects instead of playing stickball with the other guys. I came to see myself as a weak recluse – prime bully bait – whose main response to impending conflict was to run and hide.

My unclaimed power lay coiled within me like a snake that was ready to strike at the smallest insult.

TEN YEARS LATER

Kate and I are standing at the Swissair counter at the old Athens Airport. We have just cut short a holiday on the Greek island of Santorini to rush back to Zurich for a long-awaited conference with my patent attorney. And things aren't working out too well.

Our flight from the island was cancelled because of a storm. We were forced to return to Athens by overnight ferry, causing us to miss our early flight to Zurich. So here we are trying to convince the Swissair agent to accept our Olympic Airlines ticket. And we aren't making much progress.

During the intervening ten years I had learned much about conflict resolution by attending classes given by psychologist Arnold Mindell on the theory and practice of "deep democracy" and Worldwork—two new, related offshoots of his interest in applying psychological insight to working with groups and conflict. His teaching promised an alternative to the kind of "resolution" I had reached in my conflict with the hotel personnel ten years earlier – winning a victory that left everyone worse off than before. And here I was, in the midst of another conflict I needed to win.

Taking sides

Winning by overpowering my opponent, I had learned, might quickly get me to my immediate goal, but was not sustainable. It set the stage for escalation, vengeance, and even violence. Winning was not bad, but the victory would be sweeter if my "opponents" liked, or at least respected, me after the dust settled. And one of the best ways to get my opponents on my side was to show them that I could be on theirs.

Back at the Swissair counter, I listened to the agent's explanation of why he couldn't honor my Olympic ticket. I told him I felt for him. Although it seemed he had all the power, I understood that he was the victim of an uncaring and impersonal corporate power structure. I understood he was a good person in an uncomfortable role. Then I explained my position to him. I absolutely needed to get to Zurich for a business meeting. I had endured seasickness and the stink of diesel fuel all night, knowing I would probably miss a very important meeting.

According to my theoretical understanding, he should, at this point, have responded in kind by taking my position, just as I had taken his. But no such thing happened. He merely repeated what he had said before, that he couldn't accept my ticket.

That's when I nearly threw all my learning to the winds. I felt my blood pressure rising along with my tone of voice. My face started getting red. I was about to pop my cork. And then I realized I had missed something. He said he couldn't help us. That must mean that, despite the fact that he seemed to have all the power, he really did feel powerless. He didn't see himself in the same light I saw him.

And then I did something very strange. I leaned across the counter, and said to him in a confidential tone of voice, "Your balls are bigger than you think they are!" He looked shocked. Then he stood up straight. Was he going to hit me? Had I insulted him? He stepped out from behind the counter, put on his jacket, and said, "Follow me!" He led us to the Olympic counter, had a brief discussion with an agent there, and handed us new tickets. He smiled, shook our hands, and said, "Have a wonderful day."

I won, but so did he. He came away from that conflict with an expanded view of himself, as well as his own power. It was truly a "win-win" situation.

BEFRIENDING CONFLICT

Experiences like that gradually changed my attitude toward conflict. I was becoming less afraid of it, seeing it more as a playground for experiencing my own power in a way that also helped others experience theirs. I was taking the first stumbling baby steps toward making conflict an ally – even a friend – in getting closer to my own path through life. I did not know it at the time, but these two experiences showed me a direction that would later be of inestimable value in all sorts of situations, from the personal to the collective, to fields as unexpectedly wide ranging as business management and psychiatry.

Conflict could be something from which we flee. It could be something to which we get addicted as a way of satisfying our thirst for power. Or we could befriend conflict as an ally on the path of personal and social development. It is to this third alternative that this book is devoted.

CONFLICT: FRIEND OR FOE?

Conflict – whether a simple argument with a friend, or an international dispute – has enormous power for positive transformation. An argument can bring new and creative thoughts to light. A good fight, conducted fairly with opponents of comparable strength, is a great way for two people or groups to get to know each another. Even wars, despite the horror, death and destruction they leave in their wake, may leave the world better off in some ways than before they started. Many of the strongest, spiciest, and enduring relationships, from the personal to the international, start with a well-handled conflict.

But this potential is seldom realized. A funny thing happens on the way to conflict – as often as not, we are submerged in a sea of emotions that threatens to defeat us before we ever face an actual opponent. Emotions, when unprocessed, cloud our minds and possess our hearts. They blind us to our own power, and inflate the apparent power of our opponents. When conflict finally erupts, it takes place as if in a dream, autonomous and unstoppable. It may end in seemingly irretrievable acts of violence, or cycle viciously for generations.

Common ways to deal with emotions in the midst of conflict are to try to put them aside, or to use them strategically as a tool for gaining advantage over our opponents. But the emotions that precede conflict can, when treated with respect and curiosity, be so much more. They can be the very key that unlocks conflict's full potential for deepening our relationships and enriching our lives.

Emotions, when processed with curiosity and compassion, can help us to avoid escalation by revealing to us the full scope and depth of our own strength and power, regardless of how strong our opponents appear. And when we can penetrate to their core, emotions can take us straight to the very roots of our differences, revealing our common interests and values, and interrupting the cycles of half-finished conflicts that can – and often do – grip families for generations, and whole nations for centuries.

Conflict's potential for positive transformation is the strongest reason for befriending it. But there are other reasons for befriending conflict. Because conflict can be hazardous, in the balance, we may decide to forgo its potential benefits to avoid the high cost of failure. Befriending conflict opens new paths for processing conflict while minimizing its risks and dangers. One way it does this is by helping us face, rather than avoid, persistent and even threatening conflict.

Conflict's tendency to get out of hand often makes it more attractive to avoid, rather than embrace it. The word "conflict" is frightening to many people because it summons images of escalating emotions, loss of control, and ultimately, violence and destruction. When conflict goes wrong, we stand to lose our most valued relationships, our property, our status, and even life itself. This negative potential of conflict often leads us to avoid it altogether, even though we know that avoiding conflict seldom makes it go away.

On the contrary, avoided conflict goes underground, emerging in the form of both outer and inner tensions. It simply will not leave us alone. We need to live with our neighbors, both local and international. We must get along with our families, our partners, and our colleagues. Like it or not, we are inextricably entangled with one another on many levels, from the way we associate and deal with one another, to our dreams, to our fundamental human and earthly natures as social beings.

Suppressed conflicts intrude into our lives in ways ranging from persistently sour moods all the way to world-threatening cold wars. And suppressing conflict leaves us in a state of inner uncertainty. We find ourselves rehearsing the avoided conflict in our minds, going over and over various options, strategies and outcomes. We write, rehearse, and rewrite the scripts of conflict, be they for past conflicts gone awry, conflicts we are avoiding in the present, or conflicts we must face in the future.

Suppressed conflict's ability to intrude into our lives makes befriending it a good idea. If conflict keeps poking its nose into our lives, we'd best improve our relationship to it.

Although we may sidestep many of the minor conflicts that constantly jump into our path, sooner or later we will find ourselves involved in one that we can't avoid.

Whether it is a boundary dispute with a neighbor, an argument about who was responsible for a fender-bender, or a nasty divorce battle, we all find ourselves involved in conflicts from which we can't just walk away. Befriending conflict helps you be the best you can be in the worst of situations – to stay clear, present, related, and humane through even the most trying of times.

Befriending conflict improves its gain-to-pain ratio by ensuring that whether we win or lose our immediate position, we win a greater sense of relationship, security, and peace of mind. By befriending conflict, we make our opponents into allies, even if they never become our friends.

THE PATH TO BEFRIENDING CONFLICT

The path to befriending conflict starts with the knowledge that all of us – no matter what our station in life – have the resources to make the best out of the most challenging outer challenges. This knowledge is no pipe dream – it is founded upon experiences I have shared with hundreds of people I have known and worked with over more than a quarter century, from the far corners of the world and from all walks of life, in some of the nastiest and most persistent conflictual situations.

Almost everyone tells a similar story. They start off consumed by yearning – for victory, for justice, for revenge in the outer conflict. But in addition to their actual outer opponents, they come up against a host of challenges – inner challenges that diminish their clarity and power before they ever engage their outer opponents.

These challenges are far from abstract — they play themselves out as an inner drama, in which we confront our opponents and rehearse strategies for grappling with them.

Unfortunately, these rehearsals often seem to be fruitless repetitions of a single scene, going nowhere, ending in deadlock or defeat. They seem so real that we forget that all the actors in this drama, no matter how closely they resemble outer opponents, are aspects of our own fantasy, productions of our own mind.

An essential step on the road to befriending conflict will therefore be to study the inner theater of conflict with a view toward making it more of a "dojo" — a martial arts studio in which we can practice and hone our skills — rather than an early-morning battlefield of self-defeat. This will be the topic of Chapter 5, "The Inner Theater of Conflict".

But before we discuss the inner theater, I will introduce you, in the next chapter, to three of the most common challenges to befriending conflict, since these supply the concrete themes and material with which we typically fill the dramas played out on that inner stage:

Getting to know your opponent as an aspect of yourself. Since we engage in our inner dialogs with an imagined opponent, no matter how closely he resembles the outer-world opponent, he is still a product of our own fantasy. By developing a relationship to, and some detachment from this inner opponent, we begin to use it as an ally rather than as one more agent of our impending defeat. Otherwise, when we eventually engage in the outer conflict, we may find ourselves opposed by not only one but two opponents − the inner and the outer. We will introduce the concept of inner opposition in Chapter 3, and expand upon ways of befriending inner opponents in Chapter 6.

Finding out how impending outer conflict reawakens memories of conflicts past and fears of future conflicts that were there before your outer opponent ever showed up on the scene. I call these memories and fears the "ghosts of conflict", since they are ever-present but nearly impossible to pin down. Instead, they haunt our thoughts and fantasies, draining our power and pushing us toward defeat. We will introduce the ghosts of conflict in the following chapter, and explore ways of "busting" these ghostlike patterns in Chapter 7.

The third challenge is finding a source of power in yourself that does not depend on your opponent's (or anyone else's) strength. Conflict is often experienced as a win-lose proposition − a zero-sum game in which only one of the opponents benefits. By finding a source of power that cannot be taken from us, we gain clarity and new perspectives on the immediate conflict, which enable us to engage our opponents in safer, more humane ways. We will introduce this concept in the following chapter, and expand upon it in Chapters 8 and 9.

Having explored the main challenges to befriending conflict, we turn, in Chapter 10, "Practicing Safe Conflict," to the connection between power and escalation. We follow a number of examples of conflict that show how underestimating our own power leads us to over-react to an opponent — calling forth ever more powerful moves from the other side. The result is a spiral of ever-increasing power, ending in psychological or physical violence — the most feared consequence of conflict. We learn how to use the prospect of escalation as a cue to examine our own power and our own "bottom line" values as a guide to keeping ourselves and our opponents safe, while still looking out for our own interests.

And for those of us who enjoy conflict too much . . .

Chapter 11, "Itching For a Fight," examines the flip side of conflict — its addictive nature. As much as we try to avoid conflict, we turn to it in movies and TV for excitement and entertainment. And once engaged in conflict, we may be tempted to "let it rip" — to bathe in the adrenaline rush of emotion and physicality of a good fight. By keeping our awareness focused on our ultimate goal in conflict — be it justice, security, contentment, or recognition — we can decide when this goal is best served by continuing conflict, and when by sometimes more difficult person-to-person relationship.

Chapter 12, "Taking It on the Road," shows, through real-life examples, how the skills we have practiced in the preceding chapters can be applied to actual outer conflict. To illustrate this, we focus on mutual accusation, such as the ubiquitous "he started it," the most basic element that is found in all conflict, from spats between children to global warfare. We learn a very simple but effective technique for turning cycles of mutual accusation into close relationships of mutual understanding.

PRACTICE, PRACTICE, PRACTICE

Befriending conflict takes practice. Fortunately, much of it is practice you can do on your own, without ever engaging in a "real" or outer conflict. That is because a large part of befriending conflict starts with your own inner world – what I earlier called its "dream like" aspect that plays out in the inner theater of conflict.

To help you with this practice, I conclude this, and the following eight chapters, with exercises that help you explore your inner world of "conflict dreaming". Each exercise is meant to help you identify and work through the steps to befriending conflict that I explain in the body of the chapter.

In order to make the exercises clearer, I have devised an imaginary friend whose life is filled with a range of conflicts that are typical of those you and I might encounter in our personal, social, and professional lives. I've called her Janice. Her "story" is made up of events and characters that are typical of the hundreds of real people I've helped untie the knots of everyday conflict over the past 30 years. After presenting each exercise, I'll show you how Janice might work through the steps. This will help illustrate the intent behind each step, and prepare the way for you to try the exercise on your own.

After introducing you to Janice, we'll end this chapter with an exercise to help you track your current world of actual and potential conflicts. I recommend using this exercise to start a "conflict journal" that you update as you work your way through this book. That way you'll have plenty of personal material for working on the exercises in the following chapters.

So before presenting the exercise, let's meet Janice.

JANICE

Janice is 36 years old. She is a social worker in a child and family services agency. Despite the stifling difficulty of her job, she retains a good measure of the hopeful idealism that led her to choose her profession in the first place.

She was the only child of depressed and bitter parents, and she remembers the atmosphere at home as a dark cloud with a spark of fury at its core. She suffered her father's emotional remoteness and her mother's sharply critical tongue until her first year of college, when she found her way into a group of idealistic and politically radical students. She discovered that her rather grim family background gave her the authority to speak on social issues of which her more privileged fellow students had only sketchy and theoretical knowledge.

Her life is full of conflict, both actual and potential. She is divorced, with a 16-year-old daughter, for whom she is the primary caregiver. She finds herself fighting frequently with her daughter, who she feels is getting too wild for her own good. She fears for her daughter's safety. Janice has strong disagreements with her ex-husband, who she feels is too permissive of their daughter's excesses.

Janice also has conflicts with her co-workers. Where she is idealistic, she finds them jaded, going through the motions of their jobs with little regard for the humanity of the agency's clients. And being critical of her fellow social workers, she often acts aloof and superior in her dealings with them. She feels oppressed by her boss, whom she experiences as a bully. She frequently finds herself in the position of wanting to bend the rules to defend her clients' interests, but is afraid of her boss's power. She fears for her job if she stands up too strongly for her clients. At the same time, she is afraid that if she bends the rules too much, her boss may take it out on her clients, who are less able than she to defend themselves.

Despite the difficulties of her life and job, Janice remains optimistic, buoyed by her strong sense of social justice and her love of the kids with whom she works. They remind her of herself as a teenager, when she was able to use her courage and intelligence to lift herself out of the depressed atmosphere of her family. She has a realistic, rather than romantic, view of relationships. She is interested in befriending conflict because she sees its potential for putting her and her clients in better touch with their own power for survival and happiness.

TAKING STOCK OF YOUR CONFLICTS

You can refer back to this "inventory" of conflicts when you are looking for experiences on which to work in the exercises in the following chapters.

Keep a journal of your world of conflict. Make a list of the conflicts in your life – including those you call disputes, arguments, and the like. For each one, include the following information (although when Janice goes through the exercise at the end of the chapter, she will go through these steps for only one of her conflicts, to show how the steps work.)

1. **What's it about?** What are the positions or viewpoints in the conflict?
2. **Who is your opponent?** What is your relationship to them (boss, colleague, partner, relative, etc.)? What power, if any, do they have over you?
3. **What do you stand to lose?** What is at stake? What do you and the other person stand to lose? What would be the consequences of ignoring this conflict or losing it by default?
4. **What are its history and future?** Is the conflict past, present, or likely to emerge in the future? Perhaps it spans two or even all of these. How long has it been going on? How long do you expect it to last?
5. **How severe is it?** On a scale of 1 (very mild) to 7 (very severe), how strong is the conflict?
6. **Does it follow a pattern?** Is this conflict one of a kind, or is it part of a pattern of similar conflicts you've had in your life?
7. **What makes it unfriendly?** What is the most unpleasant aspect of the conflict?
8. **What makes it unsafe?** Have you gotten hurt, or have you hurt someone else in this conflict? Does it have the potential for becoming dangerous?
9. **What do you stand to gain?** If you could conduct the conflict safely, what would be its potential benefits for you? For your opponent?
10. **In balance, what's for and against befriending this conflict?** Considering 5, 6, and 7 together, what speaks in favor of going into the conflict? What speaks against it?

JANICE: MY WORLD OF CONFLICT

"I've identified several important areas of conflict in my life. In my initial survey of my conflicts, I rated each according to its severity and importance. After listing them, I'll take the most important one and go through the steps of the exercise."

I have an ongoing problem with a co-worker, another social worker who neglects his responsibilities. He keeps incomplete and sloppy case records, which I depend on for information about families with which we both have to deal. I've made several mistakes based on these records that got me into trouble with my boss. This one is mostly irritating, and I'm learning about how to protect myself from his mistakes.

I have a conflict with my daughter. She just doesn't listen to me any more. I've seen enough kids wreck their lives with drugs, pregnancy, and violence that I want desperately to protect her. But she doesn't appreciate my concerns, she just accuses me of trying to control her life. I guess this is what all mothers of teenage kids go through. Remembering my own rebellion against my mother helps get me through the worst of her outbursts.

My ex-husband is a first-class pain in the neck. Even though we're divorced, we keep fighting about how to raise our daughter. He's a charming, irresponsible SOB who uses all that charm to undermine my attempts to keep her safe.

This reminds me of my battles at work. Maybe working on one of these will help with the others.

I'm in the midst of a cold war with my boss that's about to turn hot. Some of the agency's policies really push my buttons. My conscience and my heart don't let me treat our clients as coldly as the rules require. I know my boss didn't write the rule book, but he sure sticks close to it! I feel like he's more interested in kissing up to his boss than he is in protecting our clients. And there's a storm brewing. There's one kid who's about to turn 18 and be moved from juvenile into adult jurisdiction – and I'm afraid that will be the end of him. I want to find a way to keep working with him, but my boss insists that I give him up. I feel a showdown coming that could cost me my job. I think I need to work on this one.

This last one seems the most acute. So I'll go through the exercise for my upcoming confrontation with my boss.

What's it about? My boss and I disagree on how to deal with this client. He wants to trust the system's ability to deal with the client and pass him on to adult jurisdiction. I'm afraid that would be the client's undoing.

What do I stand to lose? I feel that my relationship with the kid is the only stable thing in his life, and that losing that relationship will put him at even greater risk than he's at now. But beyond the risk to this particular client, I feel that there's an even bigger principle at stake. I feel like I'm fighting a war of hope against cynicism. Most of us social workers start off as idealists but get beaten down by the realities of the system. I feel my boss has given up too much too quickly. If I lose this one, I'm afraid I'll follow in his footsteps.

What are its history and future? This conflict has been smoldering for the past few months, but is about to erupt into the open. Although the immediate situation will come and go, the basic problem has been around as long as there have been social workers.

How severe and important is it? The conflict is severe. It is a 7 on my scale. If I either ignore it or lose it, I'm afraid I'll get horribly depressed, and become like the most cynical of my colleagues.

Does it follow a pattern? When I reflect on my role in this, it reminds me of the other conflicts in my life. I always seem to be taking on more responsibility than any one else around, and then I get in trouble for it. It's like with my parents, when I felt I was responsible for cheering them up through the worst of their depressions.

What makes it unfriendly? I hate this conflict because it brings out the worst in me. I lose my perspective. I get on my high horse and get sarcastic and down-putting with my boss. I treat him like an idiot, although I know he has a lot of the same concerns that I do. And at the same time I beat myself up for not being able to do more for this kid. I feel that if he falls, it will be because of my own failure to help him.

What makes it unsafe? This conflict is unsafe for me because I'm afraid of losing my job. And I'm mad enough to really let loose on my boss, and knowing him, that won't be good for my career. He'll get hurt, I'll get hurt, and in the end, the kid might bear the brunt of our battle.

What do I stand to gain? If there is a way to do this "right," we could all benefit. My boss and I could find a creative solution for this one kid. But more than that, we might find a way of cooperating to recommend changes in the rules that would be good for everyone.

In balance, what's for and against befriending this conflict? All in all, I think this one is worth pursuing. If I give it up now, I'll be sacrificing the core values that attracted me to this job in the first place. And that would be worse than getting fired. So let's go for it!"

THREE CHALLENGES - AND THREE KEYS - TO BEFRIENDING CONFLICT

As we start down the path toward befriending conflict, we immediately meet three inner challenges before we ever come near our opponents: the need to befriend our inner opponent, befriend the ghosts of conflict that we harbor, and recover our source of inalienable power. These three challenges have little to do with our opponents and everything to do with ourselves. We can't – and shouldn't try – to solve our conflicts by going into our bedroom and staring at our navel – far from it. But we can work on ourselves to prepare for conflict, so that we can approach it with a clear mind, an open heart, and the certainty that we are bringing all of our power to the goal of engaging in a clean fight with a worthy opponent.

Each of these challenges, like conflict itself, has both inner and outer faces. In conflict, we are often our own worst enemy, defeated by our ruminations and self-accusations before ever engaging our true opponent. We hand over the castle without a single shot being fired, or we start firing before we know who we're really fighting. We may begin to experience our own mind as an enemy. But we can befriend these inner experiences precisely because they are our own experiences. We can learn to explore and "dance" with them, free from the risks that surround outer conflict. If we can rise to the challenge posed by each of these experiences, we can prepare for upcoming conflict knowing that we've done all we can to ensure a fair and clean fight.

In this chapter, we will take a first look at these three challenges. We will first explain what they are and where they come from, and then practice identifying them in typical conflict situations from our personal and professional lives. In the following chapter, we will take a closer look at the trance-like altered states that these three challenges can provoke in us, and look at some first aid measures for restoring our mental clarity and emotional balance when we get "triggered" by these challenges.

Challenge of the inner opponent

We go over the conflict in our mind, endlessly confronting an imaginary view of our opponent. We play out various scenarios, most of which end in our defeat. If we ever confront the actual outer person, we bring along the inner version we've been imagining. So we wind up fighting both an inner and an outer version of the same guy. It is two of them against one of us—an unfair fight from the start. The challenge is to recognize the inner opponent as a reflection of our own unrecognized but potentially accessible power. Waking up to our inner opponent as an aspect of ourselves helps us confront the outer opponent with fresh, unbiased, and even compassionate clarity.

I sometimes buy a gadget, like an accessory for my computer, that doesn't do what the advertising says it should. I know the store's policy is to take it back without any justification, but I always find myself rehearsing a confrontation with a suspicious salesperson or manager. By the time I get to the store, I am feeling defensive and angry. If the actual salesperson happens to challenge me even a little, like by asking the innocent question "Why are you returning this?" I am likely to get loud and sarcastic, even though they're already processing the return. Once, while trying unsuccessfully to install a computer gizmo, I caught myself arguing with a fictitious salesperson who, in my mind, was asking me if I'd read the instructions. I noticed myself getting defensive, but then thought, "Hmmm . . . maybe he's got a point." And indeed, I read the instructions and realized that I'd been so busy attacking myself that I'd missed an important step. That inner critical voice turned out to be a valuable advisor once I'd gotten past my bruised ego. Now, when I do return stuff, I'm more confident that I've done everything I can to make it work, and I experience the salespeople as being less challenging and more cooperative.

CHALLENGE OF THE GHOSTS OF CONFLICT

We anticipate entering a conflict, only to be swamped by images of past defeats and unsatisfying victories. The ghosts of conflict past conspire with the current situation to defeat us before we start. Our challenge is to reduce the hypnotic power of the ghosts of conflict – to bring them into the light so we can see their faces and deal effectively with them in the present. Then we can be sure, when we confront our actual opponent, that we are engaged in this conflict, as free as possible from the ghosts of conflicts past and imagined.

My friend Janice – we met her in the previous chapter– found herself angry at her daughter for coming home from a date several hours later than the agreed-on time the night before. Janice knew she had to lay down the law – her daughter had been taking shameless advantage of her in recent months – but found herself paralyzed by a dreamlike memory of a similar scene between her and her mother, years before. Janice was caught between siding with her daughter and needing to set limits.

When she realized this, she was able to moderate her anger and instead become firmly factual about what she expected from her daughter. By catching the ghost of the old conflict with her mother, she was able to avoid passing it on to the relationship with her daughter.

We will have much more to say about spotting and busting the ghosts of conflict in Chapter 7.

CHALLENGE TO FIND A SOURCE OF INALIENABLE POWER

In each of these scenarios, the person's preoccupation with an inner dialog robbed them of the power to fruitfully pursue the outer conflict. Finding ways to make these inner rehearsals more useful helped them recover wasted energy and make their conflicts friendlier.

But in addition to the power we recover by dealing with inner opponents and ghosts, each of us has a deeper, more reliable source of personal power that is our birthright and cannot be taken from us by either inner or outer opponents.

Mahatma Gandhi, Martin Luther King, Jr., and Nelson Mandela are all recognized for helping some of the most disempowered people of the world find sufficient inner strength to free themselves from centuries of overwhelming oppression. Each man had his own strategy. Gandhi emphasized the equalizing power of the spirit. King emphasized the equalizing power of dreams. And Mandela emphasized the equalizing power of dignity and forgiveness. They all downplayed the importance of hierarchical power — the idea that greater power enables the strong to dominate the weak — recognizing that it is ultimately divisive, rather than unifying. They showed instead how power could be a creative force that can free us from domination and disenfranchisement. They all recognized that beefing up hierarchical power could lead only to a reversal of roles — in which the oppressed become free by becoming oppressors — and the perpetuation of the social ills that they were fighting.

Gandhi, intent on leading India toward independence from British rule, was faced with the challenge of inspiring the seemingly powerless population to nonviolently resist its masters. Although military and economic power was in the hands of the British, Gandhi knew that the deeper source of personal power lay in the ancient spiritual tradition that was the birthright of every Indian, whether Brahmin or untouchable. Gandhi saw – and identified – each of India's people as a "child of God," putting them in touch with a source of spiritual power, with its accompanying self-esteem and self-reliance, that was independent of any outer oppression.

Searching for the source of our inalienable power is a privilege because it makes us hard to beat in a conflict – but it is also brings with it the responsibility to go clear to the root of that power. Stopping halfway can be hazardous, because underestimating our own power is perhaps the most important factor that makes conflict dangerous.

That's right – I said underestimating our own power is dangerous! That needs some explanation.

It's clear that underestimating our opponent's power is dangerous. That is how wars are lost. But underestimating our own power is how wars are started, and it is responsible for everything from bullying in the schoolyard and work-place, all the way to global escalation of international con-flict. In Chapter 8, where we will take a closer look at the role of power in both starting and managing conflict, I will show how underestimating our own power is the origin of bullying – "taking it out" on someone weaker than our-selves, instead of grappling with the opponent we really need to confront. In Chapter 9, we will see how underesti-mating our own power leads to escalation of even minor conflicts. In Chapter 10, we will see how underestimating our own power makes conflict less safe than it could be, both for ourselves and our opponents. There we will see how finding a reliable connection to the source of our power can take us a giant step toward befriending conflict and getting the most goodies from it while minimizing our risk. And finally, in Chapter 11, we will see how underestimating our own power can even make conflict addictive, prolonging it far past the point where it can be productive.

FACING THE THREE CHALLENGES
WITH AWARENESS

Each of these challenges can make conflict both unpleasant and unproductive. Nothing is more depressing than facing an opponent when you are pre-programmed for defeat. Why bother? Far better to avoid the conflict or to give up before you start.

On the other hand, why should these inner rehearsals of conflict spoil the fun? There are ways to make them more productive, so that we can approach conflict with a fresh viewpoint, unburdened by the ghosts of conflict past and future.

Grappling with these three challenges will give us three keys to unlocking the mysteries of conflict. It is our task in the next several chapters to craft the first three keys to befriending conflict.

The following exercise will guide you through discovering and identifying the challenges to befriending several of your current or impending conflicts. This will prepare us for the next chapter, in which we will examine *why* these three challenges are so challenging. And we will find the answer in the power of these challenges to alter our state of consciousness in ways that block access to the very resources that could make conflict safer, more productive, and more fun.

EXERCISE:
THE THREE CHALLENGES TO BEFRIENDING CONFLICT

1. **Choose a conflict situation from the conflict journal you prepared at the end of Chapter 2.** Take one that carries an emotional charge for you.

2. **What sorts of emotional states, trances, or disturbing states of mind do you tend to get into when you think about this particular conflict?** Simply make note of these – we'll be working explicitly with these "states" in the exercise in the next chapter.

3. **Remember if and how you prepare inwardly for this situation.** Is your inner preparation effective? Or does it tend to "cycle," visiting the same problems again and again without resolution? What do you imagine would help you to prepare more effectively for the outer situation?

4. **How true to life is your imagination of your outer opponent?** Do you tend to imagine your opponent as more or less powerful than he or she acts in the outer situation? Is this type of opponent familiar to you from other conflicts? From what source do you imagine this type of opponent derives his or her power?

5. **What sorts of other remembered or anticipated conflict situations haunt your imagination of this conflict?** What makes them so powerful? Were you unable to defend yourself at the time? Are they perhaps family or even cultural ghosts that make you doubt your ability or courage to engage in outer conflict?

6. **Remember a situation in which you felt sufficiently powerful to deal with this sort of conflict.** How did you experience that power? For some it is a body experience, for others a spiritual experience, for still others a deep knowledge of an inner resource that cannot be influenced by outer experience. Imagine bringing that sense of power to the current conflict. How might it help you get through it?

Let's see how Janice approaches these questions. Then we'll move on, in the next chapter, to explore how conflict gives rise to trances and other unpleasant states of consciousness, and what sorts of strategies can help us regain our clarity when conflict looms.

JANICE: CHALLENGES TO BEFRIENDING MY CONFLICT WITH MY CO-WORKER RAY

"I have a problem with this guy Ray, a colleague of mine at the agency. I mentioned our conflict in the inventory in the second chapter. Here's the deal:"

The situation: Ray is a pig. His case records, when he bothers to keep them, are worse than useless. It would just be his own business, except several times I've inherited clients from him and then looked like an ass when I had to start all over again getting information from them — information that was embarrassing to my clients and that should have already been in his notes!

Trances and other unpleasant states of mind: When I see Ray coming with a file folder in his hand, I want to run for cover! Each time I need to use his case notes, I start shaking with fury. I can't think straight — I just want to squash him.

How I prepare inwardly for my conflict with Ray: When this issue comes up, I always try to calm myself. I try to talk myself into being humble and accepting him for who he is. But then I feel my blood pressure rising, and all my self-talk goes out the window. Trying to cool it just isn't working. I once really blew up at him. He acted like a whipped dog but didn't change his work habits one bit – if anything, his record keeping got even worse. I need a way to transform my rage into something more useful, without swallowing it completely.

How my "inner Ray" compares with the outer one: Actually, the outer guy is simply a sorry mess, whereas my inner version of him is downright dangerous. My inner version of Ray is *very* aggressive in his passivity. It reminds me of my daughter's "whatever" moods when I try to enforce rules. Both Ray and my daughter must feel hopelessly overpowered by me – much as I felt by my parents' depression. Ray's and my daughter's power comes from passive resistance – giving into the storm of my emotions until it blows itself out, then going back to following their own way of doing things.

What sorts of other remembered or anticipated conflict situations haunt my imagination of the conflict with Ray? Come to think of it, *I* was like Ray – and my daughter, when I was her age. I remember paying lip service to my mother's restrictions while trying desperately to escape from the dismal atmosphere at home. The power of this memory comes from the utter hopelessness of ever being able to break through my parents' depression. Whenever I seemed happy or enthusiastic, they looked hurt and then clamped down on me even harder. I must have looked as passive to them as Ray does to me. I am haunted by that old feeling that confrontation would be absolutely futile.

Remember a situation in which you felt sufficiently powerful to deal with this sort of conflict. I remember the first time I realized I could escape from my parents' depression. I had been out late with my friends, I was full of myself, and then my mother lit into me. I started going down but felt a kind of languid self-assurance, a memory of having had an outrageously good time with my friends. It was partly a physical sensation and partly a frame of mind. I felt *good* in a way that was *all mine.* For a moment, I felt invincible. No matter how she railed at me, my mother couldn't squash my new-found sense of happiness and self assurance.

When I hold on to that feeling and imagine confronting Ray, something amazing happens! Instead of just getting furious with him, I discover that I have a more humorous view of the situation. I imagine being a bit of a drama queen, telling him he *absolutely must* keep better records, *I do sooo depend on him!* Somehow, the humor lets me be more detached, and I feel I could do this in a good-hearted way. It might just defuse our power struggle a bit."

Trances and Other
Unpleasant States

Many of us are familiar with the experience of rehearsing for conflict before it starts—of encountering our inner opponents and getting flustered by the ghosts of past and anticipated conflicts. The purpose of this book is to help you make these rehearsals useful allies in preparing for real-world conflicts, rather than the futile, sleep-disturbing burdens they so often become. And the area where you can reap the greatest benefits is regaining a clear mind when your awareness has been clouded by confusion, fear, paralysis, or other unpleasant states of mind.

In an actual conflict, we need to have our wits about us if we are to be true to our own interests. When we get distracted by inner discussions and daydreams, we lose contact with our actual opponent and open ourselves up to premature defeat. Think of a poker game in which winning depends on remaining aware of the other players' bluffing. If you get absorbed in your own thoughts, you are likely to miss the twitching eyelid or slight grimace that could tell you whether the other guy has got a straight flush or only a pair of threes. If we get absorbed in our fear of losing, we sacrifice crucial awareness, and, with it, our money. Our fears become a self-fulfilling prophecy.

In addition to distracting us from awareness of outer events, excessive inner focus can also lead us into trancelike states. Many people describe this type of experience as becoming "fuzzy" or "frozen." They cannot speak, move, or think clearly before or during conflict.

We might describe such states as "being afraid" or being "paralyzed with fear." But these descriptions fail to do justice to the depth and complexity of the experience itself. Trance-like states, when we approach them with curiosity and awareness, turn out to be as varied as any other experiences. Like fine wines, they have nuances of flavor and atmosphere. These subtleties, when explored with an open and curious attitude, can help us step outside the box of conventional but limited wisdom to find novel solutions to difficult conflicts. We will find that focusing on these states – psychologists and recreational drug users call them altered states of consciousness – can help us creatively harness the inner world of experience that too often prevents conflict from being effective and satisfying. Befriending conflict starts with working on the trance states that stand in the way of more effective engagement. As we become familiar with these states of mind, we will learn how to enlist them as allies, if not outright friends.

At the very least, becoming aware of our trances as they happen can awaken us to the outer and inner realities we are facing. At their best, trance states can lead to totally unexpected, magical-seeming solutions to otherwise intractable struggles.

Let's take another look at our three challenges to befriending conflict to see how they put us into altered states of consciousness that cloud our minds and block our access to the resources we need most in the heat of conflict.

TWO AGAINST ONE: ENTRANCED BY AN INNER OPPONENT

When we bring an inner version of our opponent along with us, often more terrible and powerful than the actual person will ever be, we end up fighting two opponents simultaneously. Who can win that one? At best, we give up in despair; at worst, we come out swinging with a degree of force totally inappropriate to the outer challenge, which more often than not leads to dangerous escalation.

In a now-famous scene from the film *Raiders of the Lost Ark*, the hero, Indiana Jones, stands paralyzed while a fierce-looking opponent twirls a sword, preparing to carve him to bits. We stare, entranced, for what seems like an eternity, until suddenly our hero snaps awake, draws his gun, and shoots the other guy. Although shooting your opponent is not the best way to resolve conflicts, the sudden reversal in this scene is exhilarating. It satisfies our need to break through the paralysis or lethargy that many of us experience at the brink of conflict. Hypnotized by our opponent's "swordplay," we lose the clarity we need to take decisive action. It is a huge relief when Indiana wakes from his trance and plugs the guy.

Indiana Jones was daydreaming. If his outer opponent were really as powerful as the version in his daydream,, our hero would have been dead in a flash. Jones was up against not only the actual swordsman but his imagination of his opponent's power. He was fighting not one but two enemies, one outer and one inner.

Trances that come from inner opposition (or, for that matter, from any source) can take many forms. Some look like emotions. I may become afraid, angry, or unsure of myself just thinking about my opponent. Others are longer-term—emotions that have set like cement into persistent moods. I may brood, feeling depressed or hopeless, weighed down by a long, drawn-out discussion with my inner image of my opponent.

Another consequence of this two-against-one state is a cloudier kind of trance in which I don't know *what* I'm feeling. I just can't seem to think straight. My head feels like it's full of cotton candy. I don't remember what people say to me. It is like flying around in a fog, not knowing which way is up or down. This is one of the most unpleasant parts of conflict for all of us, especially when the outcome is important for our material or spiritual well-being. We may feel like powerless spectators at some of the most important events of our lives, like a dream in which we try to run but feel like our legs are made of lead, stuck to the ground, incapable of moving.

When I was studying for my PhD, I had a very stormy relationship with my academic advisor. He constantly criticized me for being too relaxed, for evidently enjoying my work too much. But I didn't feel relaxed – especially not in his presence! Whenever he turned his steely gaze on me after launching a fresh criticism, my mouth went dry and my thoughts slowed to a crawl. All the snappy comebacks that I'd rehearsed for just such a confrontation disappeared into a kind of soupy fog. I became increasingly unhappy when, as my studies progressed, I spent more and more time on those fruitless inner dialogues. My outer opponent and the sound of his voice in my head that ran on and on, whether or not he was actually present, ganged up on me.

The two-against-one scenario has the added disadvantage of blinding us to momentary opportunities for resolution of our conflict. We are so focused on fighting the inner opponent that we don't recognize when the tide has shifted in the outer conflict. We continue to fight long after the battle is over! At best, this is a waste of energy; at worst, it can re-ignite a fire that was just about dead.

After we recognize that we are fighting two opponents, we are in a position to deal with the only one we can really do anything about – the one within. There are many options open to us once we have discovered that inner opponent. But three-quarters of the battle is won as soon as we realize that the fight has been unfairly stacked against us, and that we can actually do something about it.

We will look at some ways to deal with the inner opponent in the Chapter 6, but for now, let's move on to consider the second hindrance to befriending conflict: fighting with ghosts.

FIGHTING WITH THE AIR: HAUNTED BY THE GHOSTS OF CONFLICT

When I say the word "conflict", whether in workshops or in casual conversations, I often see a subtle shift in people's body language, as if they are bracing themselves for an impact. Just saying the "C" word entrances us – puts us into altered states – by conjuring up scenes of remembered past and imagined future conflicts. It is as if we carry around a whole library of conflict scenarios along with their outcomes. And most are books we'd prefer to keep closed.

Past and future conflicts are like ghosts – they appear in almost-material form, just real enough to cast their spell on us, but too fuzzy to grasp and lay to rest. Just when we anticipate entering into a conflict, these scenes pop up, robbing us of the clarity of mind and vision that would help us prepare for the actual conflict that lies before us. The situation is similar to that of being ganged up on by an inner opponent, but more difficult to grasp because the opponent is so – ghostlike!

We enter into the outer conflict outnumbered, as in two against one, but this time our opponents are much more difficult to catch at their work. We are so deeply entranced that we are not even aware that the ghostly conflict we are fighting only vaguely resembles the one on the outside!

When anticipating conflict, we are likely to be deluged with memories of situations in which we were attacked, whether verbally or physically. We usually see the attacker as someone far stronger than we, making us unable to defend ourselves. The pain and misery of those situations hovers around us like thick fog, hiding the reality of the impending conflict and blocking our view of our own present power and ability to defend ourselves.

Ghosts are usually portrayed in stories and movies as fleeting apparitions that almost aren't there. Just when you try to pin one down, it disappears, only to re-appear when you're least expecting it. Ghosts put us into trances because they distract us from the "real" world by first drawing our attention—and then leaving nothing solid to look at!

I don't know if there are "real" ghosts, made of "ectoplasm" or whatever ghosts are supposed to consist of, but I know from personal experience that the spirits of others can hang around to haunt us. And those spirits, if nothing else, are the still-living memories of events and people who have had significant emotional impact on us.

My father, for instance, is a spirit who remains with me, even 15 years after his death. He was an argumentative fellow against whom it was really difficult to win a verbal sparring match. In my opinion, he used unfair tactics against his opponents (one of whom was, of course, me) when he felt he was about to be cornered. As the argument turned against him, his voice would get louder and acquire a sarcastic edge. His language would grow more colorful, and before long he was on the attack, even though he might be losing ground. And getting verbally attacked by my father was not a pleasant experience. Often, all it took was an innocent (to my mind) question to set him off – I didn't even have to argue. Because I frequently got stung by his sharp tongue, I grew timid in my discussions with him, eventually standing mute and dreamy while he lectured me about history, economics, and the right way to conduct my life.

To this day, when I argue with others whom I experience as having authority over me, I lapse into a trancelike state. I hear my voice slowing down, I stumble over words, my thoughts grow thick and viscous – precisely as though my father were right there, about to spear me with that indomitable tongue of his. But rather than just feeling powerless to do anything about it, I catch myself with my awareness! I realize that I am in the presence of his ghost, and that I can decide whether or not to remain entranced by it.

Another variant of fighting with ghosts crops up most frequently when we are anticipating or watching a conflict that doesn't involve us directly. We see two people or two groups in conflict, and we feel uninvolved and possibly superior to them. We think to ourselves, "They are idiots to be fighting over something so trivial! If that were me, I would straighten things out in a jiffy." And yet, when we are directly involved in conflict, we, too, may feel devoid of resources and powerless to solve what, to an outsider, may look like a trivial problem. In this case, the "expert" is a ghost – ever present, but unavailable when we really need him! And when we feel superior, it is often because of an inherited value system that sees conflict as the product of an inferior upbringing or lower social class. This attitude can produce a very subtle kind of altered state in which we feel strangely detached from the conflict, but also slightly anaesthetized or "numbed out". We may, at such times, catch ourselves yearning for a more dictectly emotional involvement in the conflict, so that we feel something, rather than nothing.

The fear of violence is another ghost that haunts our anticipation of conflict. It is a very poweful trance-inducer. It may play a considerable role in our ambivalence about intervening in others' conflict. Even when our ethical principles tell us we should.

Seeing two drunks fighting on the street, we give them wide berth, afraid we will be tainted or even hurt by intervening in their struggle – all the while looking down on them for their pointless fight. We are afraid to get involved because of the ghost of violence. We have far more models of conflict that ends in someone getting hurt than in the opponents' mutual enlightenment.

It can be foolish to endanger ourselves by getting involved in conflicts that don't seem to affect our interests. But I, for one, would be grateful for assistance when I am in a tight spot and need some help, support, or just reassurance to carry through with a conflict safely and humanely. I believe we could all be better Samaritans if we could intervene in conflicts safely and effectively, even when we are not directly involved.

You might think that the ghosts of conflict are merely negative remnants of the past that need to be cleared away so that we can get down to clear-headed procedures for resolving present conflicts. But the ghosts of conflict, when treated with respect and awareness, can actually provide the key to long-term, sustainable resolutions of rock-hard, entrenched disputes that span generations in cycles of revenge and counter-revenge, that seem entangled past any help. To find that key, it's necessary to recognize the ghost, face it squarely, and penetrate to the value that lies hidden in its nature. I call this procedure "ghost busting." My father's ghost, for instance, has turned into more of an ally than opponent as I've worked with it over the years.

I need more of my father's spirit – his punchiness, his sharp wit, his tenacity – but not in its raw form. I need to separate the good from the bad, the effective from the hurtful, in order to use his spirit more as an ally and less as a transfixing inner aggressor.

To fight a ghost effectively, you've got to meet it face to face, to grapple with it head-on. The key to dealing with ghosts effectively is to recognize them as parts of ourselves. Like the inner version of an outer opponent, ghosts are inner figures who inhabit my mind and body and whom I can get to know and deal with before I enter a conflict. And like an inner opponent, I can actually enlist the ghosts of conflict as allies on my side to help facilitate the outer conflict more clearly and more humanely – and more to my own advantage – than if I were fighting an army of almost-invisible ghosts while trying to focus on the outer situation. We will look at this and some other really effective ghost-busting measures in Chapter 7.

Now, let's see how rank and power contribute to trancelike states as we consider the last of the three great challenges to befriending conflict: discovering the source of our inalienable power.

OVERPOWERED AND OUTRANKED: ENTRANCED BY SUPERIOR POWER

No matter how strong your opponents may appear, you have an innermost source of power that neither your opponents nor anyone else can ever diminish. This source of power is your inalienable birthright.

When you are in contact with your inalienable power, you cannot be defeated in conflict. You can lose all your worldly possessions, but you will still remain connected to the source of life itself.

But when you lose contact with that deepest source of power, you are vulnerable to a very unpleasant and disabling state of mind. You are at risk of being entranced by others' seemingly superior power.

When you are out of contact with inalienable power, you draw your sense of power by comparing yourself to others. You rank others as being either more or less powerful than yourself. One of the consequences of this ranking is that you become susceptible to getting entranced by others' seemingly superior power and the rank that they seem to hold over you.

Most of us have had the experience of being summoned to a discussion by a parent, a teacher, the boss, or a traffic cop – anyone who had the kind of authority over us that made us feel small and helpless. A common reaction to such challenges is to feel "frozen"

Add to that the complication of having an actual *conflict* with such a powerful authority figure, and staying centered seems to be nearly impossible.

Indiana Jones's entrancement by his swordsman-opponent that we discussed at the beginning of this chapter could be viewed as a "rank trance". Jones was dealing with an inner version of his opponent, and was entranced by its apparently superior power.

Similarly, my entrancement by my father's "ghost" is also a persistent memory of how he outranked me in arguments.

Learning to deal with trance states induced by powerful opponents will help even out rank differentials, and will also help us recover from trance states due to inner opposition and to the ghosts of conflict. Although rank and authority differences are sufficient by themselves to produce profound trances in many of us, perceived power differentials also underlie many of the more complex trance-inducing scenarios that we have been discussing in this and the preceding chapter.

Inalienable power may sound very abstract and summon images of the Declaration of Independence, and my claim that it is more valuable than worldly possessions may seem intolerably lofty. Nevertheless, staying connected to inalienable power has been the key to the nonviolent resolution of some of the greatest conflicts of our times.

Inalienable power also has a direct influence on our state of consciousness. When I lose contact with my deepest source of power, I am like a leaf in the wind, being blown about by others' opinions and putting others' needs before my own. I lose my sense of self – I feel off-center, like a stranger wandering a strange land seeking a home that seems forever to elude me.

When I am in contact with a deep sense of inalienable power, I feel on-center, at home in my body and soul. Not having to worry about my sense of place and balance frees me to roll with the punches and flow with my opponent's energy.

Having grown up with an intellectually authoritarian father, I am apt to get depressed whenever I am challenged by others who seem to have thought more deeply or more perceptively about issues that are important to me. And if those others come equipped with a long list of credentials that seems to *entitle* them to the views they hold, that adds even more weight to my depression.

Many years ago, a psychologist friend invited me to spend a week at a psychiatric hospital at which he worked. He suggested I participate in a week of clinical meetings at which the staff – psychiatrists, nurses, psychologists and social workers – discussed the treatment plans and progress of various patients on the ward. Sometimes, the patients themselves were invited to the meetins to be interviewed by the head psychiatrist.

I found myself having many feelings about the way the cases were handled, as well as ideas about ways to communicate with the patients that might have eased the obvious tension that pervaded these meetings. Being young and brash, I decided to put some of these ideas into action, many of which proved very helpful. But I forgot that I was a visitor – I had no rank in the hospital, nor did I hold any professional credentials that would have entitled me to do anything with the patients.

As such things go, I soon came to the attention of the superintendent of the hospital, who summoned me to a meeting. I arrived in his office with sweaty palms, rapid heartbeat, and a dry mouth. He called on me to account for my unauthorized interference in the working of the hospital. To this day, I'm not sure what helped me maintain a degree of composure, but I recall feeling sure of what my eyes, ears and heart told me about my relationship to the patients and staff. I had, more or less unconsciously, tapped into a sense of being at home in myself – in my perceptions, ideas and beliefs. And that somehow got me past the fight-or-flight reaction that threatened to overtake me just before the interview.

Nowadays, thanks in great measure to Arnold Mindell's research into a level of experience he refers to as "sentient essence", I have access to a method that helps me rapidly gain access to what I have been calling my sense of "inalienable power". That is the subject of the following exercise. You will find that penetrating to the essence of an altered state of consciousness preceding a conflict will give you access to unexpected power that cannot be easily shaken by inner opponents, the ghosts of conflict, or outer opponents that clearly outrank you.

EXERCISE: IDENTIFYING ALTERED STATES CONNECTED WITH CONFLICT:

In the following exercise, you will review some of the altered states of consciousness that you have met in your world of past, present, and impending conflicts. You will identify the source of these states – whether from internal opposition, ghosts of conflict, or loss of contact with your source of inalienable power. You will then practice a simple method for rapidly reconnecting with that source of power to help you regain clarity and a sense of center.

1. **Review the conflict journal** you prepared in Chapter 2, being sensitive to the variety of altered states that are provoked by each of those situations.
2. **For each of the conflicts,** ask yourself if the altered state is primarily due to:
    - a conflict with an inner image of an outer opponent
    - being haunted by a ghost – a memory or fear – of past or impending conflict
    - feeling outranked by a someone with power or authority over you
3. **Recall a situation in which you felt at home in yourself,** centered, grounded, or secure in your own power, in the midst of a conflict. Focus specifically on the body sensations and posture connected with that feeling. Try to locate the feeling in your body. Go slowly. Body feelings often need more time to connect with than do images or inner voices. Make a small movement that you can later use to remind you of that feeling.
4. **Now revisit one or two of the conflicts** you examined in steps 1 and 2. As you do so, try to stay connected with the feeling of centeredness you accessed in step 3. Notice what effect this has on the altered states connected with each of these conflicts.

JANICE: MY ALTERED STATES OF CONFLICT

"I generally see myself as pretty level-headed. I don't much think about myself as prone to altered states – except, maybe, when I've had one drink too many at a party. But let's try it anyway…"

When I review the conflicts I wrote down in my journal, the only experiences that I can identify as altered states

seem to revolve around anger and frustration. I seem not to be too susceptible to getting entranced by others' power – I'm more likely to fly off the handle than to freeze up during a confrontation.

I'll consider a couple of those conflicts in detail:

In the conflict with my co-worker, I am frustrated because I know I could really demolish him, but I've lost too many friends and allies by losing my temper with them. I guess I'm being haunted by the ghosts of old conflicts that turned out badly for me.

In the ongoing conflict with my daughter, I feel overpowered by her. Whether she's guilt-tripping me, or merely accusing me of being unfair, I lose my sense of centeredness – I always leave those confrontations feeling knoced off balance.

In the conflict with my ex-husband, I always end up feeling like a frumpy old kill-joy. I keep rehearsing our arguments over raising our daughter, and keep coming out second best. I am somehow entranced by his charm, which I, as the one who's responsible for her everyday well-being, can never match. Looks like a case of being entranced by an inner opponent – I wind up furious and frustrated without ever having to speak to my damned ex!

Hmmm....feeling centered in the midst of a conflict...that's a tough one. But I do remember a time when I've went to bat for a client who I felt had been seriously wronged by the social services. I was certain that her case worker had dropped the ball. I had my facts in order, I knew I was right, and I was able to dispassionately but very strongly represent her case, and got her what she needed.

Did a body feeling go along with that? Yes. I felt like I was solidly planted in the ground. I felt, literally, like a heavy-weight, like a tree with its roots way down in the earth, like nothing could move me. A movement to anchor that feeling? I rock slightly back and forth on my heels, and can feel my weight going straight down into the ground. It's like moving in an immovable way.

When I go back and review the three situations I mentioned in step 2, I notice I'm not so easily swayed (hmmmmm!) by my opponents' power. In the case of my colleague, that's similar to the experience I mentioned in step 3, where I felt centered and confident in my position. With my daughter, I know that kind of power in her…she always seems so dead sure of herself. When I feel myself planted in the earth, I notice myself not being so impressed with her solidity. I think we could have a fair and guilt-free fight. And in the confrontation with my ex…somehow it doesn't seem important to me. From the perspective of this new stance, he looks like a leaf in the wind, held aloft by his own vanity, but without much power or conviction behind it.

THE INNER THEATRE
OF CONFLICT

The inner opponent and the ghosts of conflict…these "characters" make intuitive sense to us because we spend so much time visiting them in our inner theatre of conflict. Whatever fights we have on the outside we have rehearsed dozens, if not hundreds, of times on the stage of our minds. We either rehash old conflicts to see how they could have turned out better, or we anticipate the next round in a current or upcoming conflict.

When these practice rounds are successful, they help us learn from past experience and prepare us for coming conflict. But just as often these inner rehearsals lead us in circles, reinforcing our fears and leaving us hopeless about ever digging through the outer situation.

Our goal in this chapter is to set the stage for making these inner rehearsals more helpful, so that they have a better chance of directing us toward more effective conflict resolution. Creating helpful rehearsals would be a huge first step toward befriending conflict. It would turn any conflict into an opportunity for learning. And as we know in our hearts, a conflict from which we can learn, even if we "lose" in the conventional sense, is worth its weight in gold. Learning ho to use any particular conflict as an opportunity for learning to work with conflict in general puts a new spin on the old proverb, "Give them fish and they can feed themselves for a day; teach them how to fish, and they can feed themselves for a lifetime."

THE INNER DRAMA OF CONFLICT

"Real" theatre is performed on a stage, with actors playing roles that have nothing to do with their personal lives. The stage frames the action, showing that it's a work of art, not real life.

In order to keep our interest, theatre must reflect real-life situations and experiences with which we can identify. The more psychologically realistic the production, the more we can identify with all the characters' experiences, so that we see the entire drama – or comedy – as a mirror of our own lives, in all their tragi-comic complexity.

Effective drama also mirrors our own "inner theatre," the chorus of internal voices that supports, argues with, and criticizes the viewpoint that we take to be our own. This inner theatre can either help or hinder us in our daily activities. When its voices agree with us, we feel supported. When the voices argue constructively with us, they can spur us on to clear thought and decisive action. But when they destructively criticize our viewpoint, we begin to doubt and even hate ourselves, leaving us depressed and unable to act.

However active our inner dramas may be in ordinary times, there's nothing like an impending conflict to get them working overtime. When conflict threatens, the inner theatre plays round the clock (especially around 4 A.M.), showing us all sorts of possible outcomes, from the most favorable to the most disastrous. This display could all be very illuminating, were we not passive observers, confined to the audience, watching the drama play out on stage. And we are not even free to walk out!

Our challenge is to befriend these inner dramas rather than remaining their passive victims. Since they already carry a complete image of the upcoming conflict, they provide a terrific opportunity to practice our moves before we actually engage in the conflict.

The inner theatre of conflict is less than helpful when it simply replays and reinforces our fears and doubts, hindering rather than helping our attempts to resolve the outer situation. Inner theatre tends to circle viciously when we forget that all of its characters are different sides of our own personalities. A first step toward making the inner theatre of conflict more useful and less of a vicious circle is to bring an attitude of deep democracy toward all of its characters. Being deeply democratic means befriending all of the characters of the inner theatre as valuable parts of ourselves, even when these parts do not share our viewpoints, values, or style of relating.

DEEP DEMOCRACY AND THE INNER THEATRE

Whenever people get together as a group, whether to share a quiet evening at home or to found a new nation, they tend to form an "in-group," which, on a wider social level is called the mainstream. And as soon as there's an in-group, there are out-groups. The out-groups are the people who don't share the viewpoints, values, or goals of the in-group, and who feel themselves deprived of the benefits of membership. Out-groups are usually minorities and may be as small as one individual.

Democracy is one method for dealing with differences of opinion in a group. We take a vote, and the group that gets the most votes wins. The viewpoints of those who lose don't simply vanish, however. They crop up sooner or later as conflict.

Deep democracy is the attitude that all viewpoints in a group are valuable, meaningful, and worth considering, no matter how few people hold them. To be a deeply democratic leader, you need to cultivate the attitude that all views are important, even – or particularly – those that conflict with your own.

To lead a group in a deeply democratic way, you need to follow it with your awareness of the diverse viewpoints of its members. If you are sincerely interested in helping holders of these viewpoints express themselves, you are halfway toward becoming a deeply democratic facilitator. When a group is prepared to embrace its own diversity of viewpoints, it becomes more hospitable to all its participants. Its members feel more secure, even though considerable differences of opinion may still fuel conflict within the group.

When we rehearse conflict in the inner theatre, we are on our way toward bringing a deeply democratic perspective to the diversity of our own viewpoints. But if we experience the rehearsal as less than useful, it is because the inner conflict is not facilitated – it goes around in circles, with all participants digging in their heels and sticking to their positions, just like in most outer conflicts.

Befriending the Actors of the Inner Theatre

To make friends with people, you've got to respect their views. Otherwise you may dominate or submit to them, but you won't be their friend. People become friends when they know that it is safe to express conflicting opinions about hot topics. They know that even if they disagree, they will give each other a fair hearing. They will put the relationship first and the content of their disagreements second.

Deep democracy is a way of befriending those who hold views that conflict with your own, whether in the outer world or in your inner theatre of conflict. To see how deep democracy can help you befriend troublesome inner characters, let's take a look at a property dispute in which I was involved several years ago. Rehearsals in my inner theatre of conflict saved me from starting a vendetta with a neighbor. We will see how all three of the greatest challenges to befriending conflict initially got in my way. After opening the show by describing how the conflict came to pass, we will see, in the following three chapters, how working with inner opposition, the ghosts of conflict, and exploring the source of my inalienable power all played a part in the eventual resolution of what was, at times, a very nasty conflict.

Conflict with a neighbor

There's nothing like an annoying neighbor to give you opportunities to practice deep democracy in the inner theatre of conflict.

We got a call from a new neighbor – let's say his name is Jerry – who had recently bought a piece of land adjacent to ours. He had a plan that needed our help.

He wanted to build a house on his newly acquired lot. But his property had no direct access to the main road on which our house stands. His land was down the slope of a very steep hill right below ours. The lower boundary of his land was shared by a public park. To get access to his planned house, he needed to build a road, but the road had to cross someone else's land – either ours or the park's.

To complicate the matter, Jerry was guaranteed access to his land by "easements" – legally granted rights-of-way – one crossing our land, and one on the border of the park. But the one from the park was quite far from his planned house, a huge distance to haul building materials. And the one on our land was short but very steep and only ten feet wide.

Jerry knew that neither of his legally guaranteed access paths was very convenient – so he tried to talk us – first sweetly and then more aggressively – into letting him build a long, wide road over the main part of our property.

His plan would have divided our property in half – not a very attractive proposition for us, especially since he offered us nothing in return. When we hesitated, Jerry insisted that he had a right to the more extensive and divisive roadway. He produced aerial photographs and maps going back more than 50 years to "prove" that there had been a road there before and to imply that this "fact" gave him the right to rebuild that old road.

Jerry and I clearly had a conflict of viewpoints about what he was entitled to.

According to him, he was entitled to build a roadway over our property. His claim on our property was partly legal, based on the easement guaranteed by our deed.

We disagreed with him. We believed that the easement would not stand up to legal examination, since a roadway, in the modern sense of the word, could not be built on such a steep, narrow strip of land.

But Jerry wanted more than the law promised him. He claimed that he was entitled to rebuild the previously existing road, of which there was no legal record – only a blurred line on an old aerial photograph!

That was too much for us. We felt he was strong-arming us, partly by bluster and partly by lying. We had no evidence whatsoever of a previously existing roadway, and even if it had existed, we doubted it gave him any legal right to rebuild it.

We didn't know if Jerry had a legitimate claim on our land but we since we felt tricked and dishonored by him, we decided to stick to our guns. We even hired the scariest lawyer we could find to try to fend him off – but he kept arguing until it became clear that only a civil lawsuit would end the matter once and for all. But that was risky. What if we lost? What a pain in the neck! And what an opportunity to learn about deep democracy.

We considered escalation. We suspected that some of his building plans were illegal, but that he had treated the city permits office the same way he treated us – kept lying and hammering at them until they gave him what he wanted. We had evidence that he had lied. Why not snitch on him to the city to try to get his permits revoked?

Although I did complain to the city, I finally decided to do something friendlier. I wanted a solution that would let us live in relative harmony – and one that would let me live with myself. I felt that winning the battle wouldn't get me what I was really longing for – the right to enjoy our own home without the disturbance of people traipsing back and forth across our property.

I knew that to win, I'd need to do something really drastic. I might get my way (hmmm....what was my way? I scarcely knew by that point!), but then I'd have to live – who knows how long? – in the crossfire of a vengeful neighbor and my own bad conscience.

On the other hand, if I gave up too much, I'd be perpetually dissatisfied. I'd always be watching him to make sure he didn't encroach on our boundary lines or make too much noise at night.

WHERE NEGOTIATION DOESN'T WORK

In situations like this, it seems reasonable to negotiate. Since the legal status of Jerry's claims was unclear, perhaps he, too, would be more interested in negotiating than in a lawsuit. We could sit down together, have a rational discussion, and each give up a little something to appease the other. We might let him use the easement for emergencies, in return for his giving up any claim on the larger, more divisive roadway.

The only trouble was negotiation didn't – couldn't – work. I was too upset to just negotiate a settlement. I was offended by his invasion of our space. I felt he had already taken too much. I wasn't ready to give up anything more for the sake of peace.

Negotiation is forward-looking. It maps out a process of give and take to be carried out in the future. If one party feels the other's demands are completely unreasonable or disrespectful of its position, the negotiation becomes clouded by conflict and is unlikely to result in a sustainable outcome.

The dispute with Jerry had too much history of hard feelings. I needed a procedure that took those old hurts – the emotional side of the conflict – into account.

REHEARSING IN THE INNER THEATRE

I realized that I was spending a lot of time going over the situation in my mind. So I decided to observe myself thinking about it – I became both a participant in, and the audience to, my own inner theatre of this conflict.

In a typical scene, I would watch suspiciously while Jerry worked away at his property. I saw him as unrelenting, cheap, secretive, unemotional, and uncommunicative. In my mind, he was trying to get something for nothing, slipping under the city's radar by lying about his intentions, and then hammering away at any remaining resistance until he got what he wanted.

As a participant in the theatre – playing the role of myself, so to speak – I felt victimized by Jerry's intrusion into my life. In my role as a relatively peace-loving, accommodating fellow, I felt powerless to stop him, believing that his persistent toughness would eventually get him his way. In another sense I felt free – or at least tempted – to use whatever means I could to get my way. Those means included complaining to the city bureaucrats who were responsible for giving him permits and enlisting a nasty lawyer to challenge his right to make a path through our land.

That was the setup – the stage setting at the beginning of the drama (or would it be a comedy?). It had all the elements of a typical production in the inner theatre of conflict:

First, there was my inner image of Jerry – a tough, unemotional guy who seemed just the opposite of me. I tended to see myself as a pushover, unable to take my own side whenever physical strength counted more than the mind. And I saw Jerry as distinctly physical, a man of strong action and few words.

This image of Jerry, as well as the whole setup, brought up the ghosts of the past – countless times when I'd gotten beaten up by bullies and was unable to defend myself. I took refuge in my mind but secretly itched to "give it back" to my tormentors in kind – to teach them a lesson they wouldn't soon forget.

And finally, I realized that defeating Jerry by attacking his vulnerabilities – his tendency to lie in order to get his way, his seeming inability to deal with strong emotions –

would satisfy my need to win this fight but would not address a much deeper-seated yearning. And that was to establish myself as a stake-holder in the world itself. I had identified with my geekhood for so long, I needed to fight, again and again, with outer tough guys to prove that I could hold my own with them. But my deepest struggle was with an inner voice, inherited, perhaps, from a long family tradition, that put me down no matter what I did – an abiding sense of inadequacy that I knew could never be reconciled by defeating an outer opponent.

It seems that the three challenges to befriending conflict are not so clearly separated as I implied at the beginning – indeed, they are all part and parcel of the same basic struggle. And yet, each is significant and differs from the others when it emerges into outer conflict. Each emerges in its own time, contributing to the feeling that "one thing is piled on another" until an unmanageable heap of trouble forms. The reward of working on an outer conflict first as an inner drama is a greater sense of unity; there is a dawning recognition that challenges that seemed separate all grow from a common root. So as we explore these different facets of befriending conflict, a side effect will be a more firmly grounded sense of who we are and what we are doing on this earth. And that, in itself, will help transform conflict from a painful and dangerous threat to a sublime, though challenging, promise.

Now would be a great time to explore a conflict of your own. The following exercise gives you a series of simple steps to rehearse an actual conflict of yours in your inner theatre. To help guide you through these steps, the chapter ends with Janice exploring the inner theatre of a conflict with her daughter.

EXERCISE:
EXPLORING THE INNER THEATRE OF CONFLICT

1. **Choose, from your inventory of conflicts, a particular situation** that you keep coming back to in your mind.
2. **What are the outer facts of the conflict?** Who is your opponent? What is at stake? How severe is the conflict?
3. **Who are the characters in your inner rehearsal of this conflict?** Describe them as you experience them in your inner musings, rather than as they appear in the outer world.
4. **What typical scenes keep occurring in your rehearsals?** Where does the drama "cycle" without resolution?
5. **What does the "stage setting" look like?** Is it similar to, or different from, the usual context in which you face your outer opponent? How would you describe the atmosphere? Is it tense, scary, challenging, or, perhaps even warm and inviting?
6. **Now imagine yourself in the audience, as an observer to the conflict,** at the same time as you are watching yourself on the stage as a participant in the drama. From the standpoint of the audience, you may notice things about both yourself and your opponent that you usually don't see when you are only a participant in the drama. Pay attention to things like:
    • How powerful does your opponent look?
    • How powerful do you look, particularly compared to how you usually see yourself?
    • How do you and your opponent appear different?
    • How do you and your opponent appear similar?

• Above all, notice anything that surprises you about any of the characters or about the situation in general. What does this surprising element suggest to you about possible strategies for making the outer conflict safer, friendlier, or more productive?

Now let's see how Janice follows these steps to rehearse for a conflict with her daughter that she's been avoiding.

JANICE: REHEARSING FOR A CONFLICT WITH MY DAUGHTER

"It never rains but it pours! I get enough troubled kids in one day to last most people for a year, but then, when I get home, I've got a rebellious daughter to deal with. I've been trying to avoid trouble, but things are coming to a head. So let's give it a go."

A conflict from my inventory: My daughter is driving me crazy. She's smart, does well at school, has lots of friends, and we've gotten along really well up to now. But lately, she's acting like she can barely tolerate having me around. She's got the "whatevers."

The outer facts: She's getting wilder, more secretive. She comes home late and won't say where she's been. I'm afraid she'll get into trouble – drugs, sex, etc. – but she won't discuss it with me. She's turning into an opponent. I fear that my relationship with her is at stake. If I don't handle this right, I may lose her, if not physically, then emotionally.

Characters in the inner theatre: The main characters are my and me, with her friends playing bit parts and serving as an invisible chorus. When I focus on my imagination of what's happening — which actually feels worse than the outer situation — I see a drama unfolding in which she's out to get me. She harbors some deep, mythic grudge that she's going to exercise by pushing, pushing, pushing on whatever limits I set for her, until I finally explode, and she's vindicated. I see her friends milling around downstage silently egging her on, as she fights for the rights of the young-and-full-of-juice against depressed adult oppression.

Typical scenes: I keep seeing myself laying down the law to my daughter after she comes home very late from a party, while she stares vapidly off into space. No matter what I say, it seems to increase the distance between us, until I am really terrified that she will leave and never come back.

The stage setting: We are in front of the house. My daughter is walking toward her friend's car, her head swiveled around as if to argue with me, but then shaking her head, as if terminally frustrated, and finally facing completely away from me. She is basically intent on her getaway. The atmosphere is heavy, tense, and hopeless.

Joining the audience: Okay, now I'm going to take an outside position and watch the drama between my daughter and myself unfold.

How powerful does my daughter look? Well, very powerful. She has no idea how self-assured, physically strong, and confident she looks.

How powerful do I look? Also very powerful. But when I'm in the drama, I feel like a wimp. No matter how much I shout and stamp, I feel like I have no effect on her.

But looking in from the outside, I see just how formidable I look!

How do we look different? My daughter looks confident, whereas I look harried and disheveled. I'm close to "losing it," whereas she looks like the soul of composure.

How do we look similar? We both look like Titans – each of us very powerful, locked in a life-and-death battle.

"Surprise! I am astonished by the symmetry of the scene—each of us feeling overpowered by the other, but from the outside, looking like either of us could win a major battle. It occurs to me that if we joined forces, we could do nearly anything. Is it possible that we are fighting not to win but to learn about how strong we really are? I think that if we discussed this, or (forbidden thought) even made a video tape of us fighting and then watched it together, we would gain a new appreciation for how powerful we really are, both individually and together."

Now, we'll move on to examining each of the three keys to befriending conflict in greater detail, starting with befriending an inner opponent.

Befriending Inner Opposition

Let's take another look at my property dispute with my neighbor Jerry. When he encroached on my partner Kate's and my property, my inner conflict proved more of a stumbling block than Jerry himself. It was difficult for me to stand up for my own interests, because I was already at odds with myself.

In this chapter we will take a closer look at that situation to learn how to harness an inner opponent as an ally and reliable advisor in befriending outer conflict.

A Matter of viewpoint

From the point of view of an audience member – that's me, observing the "other" Joe duking it out with Jerry – I saw both Joe and Jerry as powerful characters.

Jerry was wiry, strong, resourceful, and tough. He and his wife had single-handedly surveyed and cleared the steep, bramble-overgrown slopes of his property. He was a bit over the top in his nature-boy insistence on collecting rainwater and composting his family's solid waste to make fuel gas (no kidding!). But he had clearly moved to our part of the city to enjoy its relative seclusion and natural beauty.

Joe (from my audience-member's point of view) was also tough and straight in his own way. When he confronted Jerry, he didn't pull any punches, nor did he fight unfairly. He looked stronger and more self-assured than I thought he gave himself credit for – and I ought to know! He was also fighting to preserve the natural beauty and seclusion of the area. He was afraid that Jerry was going to leave too large a footprint on one of the remaining wildly wooded corners of the city—which happened to be where he lived.

Looking at the two of them, I saw more similarities than differences. I saw them both as powerful characters in the prime of life. Both were in love with the natural beauty and solitude of the spot they had chosen as home. And each saw the other as a block to his full enjoyment of that spot.

Observing them from a more detached position enabled me to see more of my own power, which shifted my viewpoint slightly and freed me from feeling that I was purely a victim of Jerry's pushiness. Realizing that I was not just his victim allowed me to see the positive side of Jerry's power. I realized that I secretly admired him. He was a competent, resourceful guy, with a physical and mental toughness that I could use more of in my daily life.

Why did I secretly admire Jerry's toughness? On the surface, it seemed that if I admired him too much, I might lose my advantage over him and too easily give up my own position. But my difficulty admitting my admiration went deeper than my fear of losing a competitive advantage over him. I was actually envious of him. I felt I wasn't up to his standards. Why hadn't I surveyed and cleared our land? I would have loved to build a little house as a retreat but would never even consider doing it myself. To even try would bring up my whole personal history of feeling too weak to really grapple with the physical world "like a man." Jerry showed me a side of my personality that I preferred not to face.

And there is still one further level to this saga. I do not – cannot – know who Jerry actually is. I have never stood in his shoes or even walked down his road with him. Perhaps he gains his tough competence at the expense of others like me, who feel they can't stand up to his energy and resolve. Perhaps he suffers from his own tendency to ride over the will of others to get his way. But my inner version of Jerry is tough and resourceful in a way with which I don't identify. This resourcefulness—and toughness—must be hidden abilities that I have yet to discover in myself.

To the extent that I believe my inner version of Jerry is all about him and not at all about myself (in psychological terms, we would call this a projection), I deprive myself of the positive qualities I see in him. Whatever positive qualities I project onto Jerry, I lose for myself. I see them only in him, not in myself.

By letting the drama of Jerry and Joe play out in my inner theatre of conflict, I could begin to appreciate the outer Jerry's positive qualities as well as to recognize these qualities as belonging to me. It became a win–win situation. But I was the double winner. I had both moderated my view of Jerry – which was sure to smooth over my future relationship with him – and I had gained a more comprehensive view of my own capabilities and limitations—as well as a clear guide for a direction in which I needed to grow. Quite a harvest from a simple boundary dispute!

And by rehearsing this conflict as an inner project, I had given up nothing in the outer arena. I was free to go back into the conflict with the real, outer Jerry, but this time reinforced with a more complete view of both him and myself

BACK TO THE CONFLICT

How did my inner work affect the course of the outer conflict? After the dust had settled from our initial property wars (lawyers, examination of deeds, etc.), Jerry asked us one final time for permission to use the path through our property, "only for emergencies." We had a moderately pleasant discussion in which we each stated our needs and wants, as well as discussing our common love for the land and its natural beauty. The atmosphere of contention had all but vanished. I'm not sure what changed things on his side. I know, however, that I was no longer able to view him only (or even mainly) as an enemy. I realized that our views would never completely coincide, but it no longer seemed to matter. Since then, Kate and I have had a comfortable live-and-let-live relationship with him.

And he seldom, if ever, uses the path through our property.

Now we've had a first look at how rehearsing in the inner theatre of conflict helped me prepare for an ordinary squabble between neighbors. In the rest of this chapter, we'll see how to use that experience to prepare for any conflict by befriending inner opposition. In the following two chapters, we will befriend the ghosts of conflict and then explore the source of our inalienable power, which can help us through the most difficult of times, no matter what opposition we face on the outside.

INNER OPPONENTS

When we enter a conflict without consciously rehearsing first in the inner theatre of conflict, we are immediately outnumbered. We are fighting not only the outer opponent but also the image of him or her that we carry around in our mind. Our challenge is to befriend that inner opponent so that it becomes an ally rather than an adversary.

Why befriend it? Why not just find a way to get rid of it, so that the fight is fairer? There are two main reasons for befriending, rather than destroying, an inner opponent.

First, it is nearly impossible to get rid of an inner opponent. Although we may convince ourselves that it is only a figment of our imagination, this pesky inner opponent comes back to trip us up just when we thought we'd banished it from our lives. The inner opponent feels real to us, rather than imaginary, even though it lives only in our own mind!

A more interesting reason to befriend the inner opponent is to transform it from an adversary into an ally. An ally is not necessarily a friend — it is, however, someone with whom you share a common interest, upon whom you can rely to be on your side for the duration of the conflict. During the Second World War, the Soviet Union and the United States were allies because they had a common interest in defeating the Axis powers. But they were not friends — in fact, they became bitter enemies the moment their common goal was reached.

You don't need to like your inner opponent, but it's always a good idea to join forces with it before going into battle. In fact, the less you like it, the more important it is to have it on your side.

But who or what is this inner opponent? What makes it so persistent? And how can we go about befriending it?

The inner opponent is a blend of past experience and present beliefs about who we are and who we are not. These beliefs shape and reflect how we think and feel about ourselves and how we act toward the outer world. But they are so deeply ingrained in us that we are seldom even aware of them. They are like the smell of air or the taste of water.

GETTING TO KNOW THE INNER OPPONENT

Actually, we know our inner opponents all too well. They speak to us with the voice of our thoughts. We often overlook inner opposition because it sounds like the usual chatter that fills our heads in times of conflict. We seldom stop and say, "Wow, that thought sounded like a self-criticism! I wonder if it's worth listening to."[1]

Many of our thoughts take the form of an inner conversation or debate (sometimes called self-talk). I think,

"I'll just phone Jerry and tell him how upset I am by his plans." And then I think, "But he'll just blow me off. He's more self-assured than I am, I'll just start mumbling and excusing myself."

This seemingly simple thought is a mini-debate between two viewpoints. To consider calling Jerry to have a talk with him, I would need to feel myself more his equal. But to conclude, ahead of time, that he will blow me off and be more self-confident than I am, I must think of him as the stronger, more powerful person. Two viewpoints are locked in a debate. Which one will win?

If I try to ignore the second voice, the one that says I'm weaker, I might call Jerry but be dragged down by self-doubt. I will spend my time listening to that second voice taking Jerry's side against me. It will be two against one, and I will probably sound like a fool and act like a push-over. And I will not know from where that inner opposition, which feels like sabotage, is coming.

When I am unaware of that opposing inner viewpoint, I am too vulnerable to its almost unheard whisperings in the midst of my valiant attempt to win the fight with Jerry. On the other hand, if I pay too much attention to the voice that tells me I am weaker than Jerry, I may never make the call. I may forget the first viewpoint that thinks I'm a pretty good match for him. I am defeated before I start.

When I realize that my rehearsal of a phone call to Jerry really has two viewpoints, parts, or roles, I am on the road to winning back my power. I am no longer just a victim of the image of Jerry I carry with me as an inner, critical voice. Just noticing the critical inner voice restores my power, because I am no longer undermining myself unconsciously.

WHERE THE INNER OPPONENT GETS ITS POWER

What makes this inner opponent so powerful? Why does simple self-talk have such a big effect on us? Why can't we just ignore it?

For one, it keeps on talking, even when we wish it wouldn't. Just wanting it to go away usually won't turn it off.

Even when we can't banish that voice, recognizng inner opposition by saying, "Hello, there you are again!" can reduce its sting.

But realizing that we are talking to ourselves is only a beginning step. That critical voice still has the power to distract us from the outer task. Just like a real outer person who keeps pestering us even after we try to shut him or her up, it's enough to drive us crazy. Constant, demoralizing, self-critical talk leaves us feeling flat and defeated before we even start talking to an outer opponent.

But why won't that critical voice go away? Why can't we reason with it, put it on hold, send it out for a cup of coffee while we sit and collect ourselves before the outer battle? Because the voice of inner opposition has a legitimate message. Its voice expresses one viewpoint among many that we have about ourselves. And because the viewpoint is legitimate, it won't go away just because we wish it to. It is a real and important part of a sober self-evaluation.

That critical voice is difficult to listen to because it is one-sided. It sounds like it is trying to destroy us, even though the information it gives us may be valuable, even crucial, to knowing ourselves more fully.

Befriending the inner opponent is therefore a tricky business. To befriend that critical inner voice, we need to discover and appreciate its value. And then we need to teach it to deliver its valuable information in a friendlier way.

Viewed from another angle, grappling with that inner opponent can lead to not only more effective outer conflict resolution, but also lay the groundwork for a rich and reliable path to genuine self-love. We cannot embrace ourselves totally unless we can include those inner voices that point the way toward more empowerment, effectiveness, and self-assurance. The trick is to recognize the intent behind the sometimes rough exteriors of these inner critics and to find a way to take in the information while still being kind to ourselves.

BEFRIENDING THE INNER OPPONENT

Here is a new concept: Inner opposition is not all negative. But like any other voice that has been suppressed for too long, it gets a bit nasty.

One reason we have learned to reject inner criticism is because it sounds too much like the unfriendlier side of those parents, teachers, and siblings who put us down as we were growing up. We are suffering from generations of (hopefully) well-meant but poorly delivered advice that often cut us down way too low instead of encouraging us to use all our strength and intelligence to reach new heights. Many of those critical voices came from a harsh style of education that thought it better to emphasize our weaknesses than our strengths. Criticism that could have strengthened us with useful self-knowledge instead became a bitter pill that weakened us with self-doubt.

In order to befriend inner opposition, we need to separate the wheat from the chaff, so to speak. We must sort out the good advice from what merely puts us down.

An important step for dealing with these voices is to turn toward them instead of away from them – to take them seriously – to recognize that they won't go away on their own. We need to respect them and relate to them. If we can take inner criticism seriously, it begins to lose its sting, just as recognizing an outer tyrant's power is a first step toward building a diplomatic relationship with him. Taking inner opponent seriously is an important step along the path to building a relationship with it.

Finally – and this step is useful in any conflictual situation – we need to find a reliable source of inner strength, so that we can stay centered while considering the value of critical inner voices.

SEPARATING THE WHEAT FROM THE CHAFF

Wheat has nourishing kernels, full of protein, carbohydrates, oils, and vitamins. The kernels grow in fibrous husks, the chaff, which is impossible for us humans to chew, much less digest. To get the goodness out of the wheat, we've got to separate it from the chaff.

Inner opposition can be nourishing in its core, but it, too, is covered by irritating and unpalatable negativity. Our challenge is to separate the nourishing from the merely irritating in our inner theatre of conflict.

Jerry's pushiness and lack of feeling for our situation made whatever goodness he had difficult to appreciate. In order to benefit from his positive qualities, I needed to first defend myself against the negative.

I did this by becoming an audience member in my inner theatre of conflict – by separating myself from my role as just Jerry's counterpart. From the cooler detachment of an observer, I was free first to see my own positive qualities – I was neither as incompetent nor as weak as I tend to see myself. And then I was able to appreciate the qualities I admired in Jerry, but had not dared admit, for fear of trashing myself through the comparison.

Finally, I was able to appreciate what Jerry – at least, my inner version of him – and I shared, freeing me to see him as an ally as well as an opponent. And this last act of awareness released enough tension in the outer conflict to allow me to meet with him and negotiate a mutually agreeable solution.

TAKING INNER OPPOSITION ON BOARD

When you have found a stable base from which to defend your own viewpoint, you will be in a better position to start listening to your inner opponent's opinions. You are on your way to converting your inner opponent into an ally.

Here are some frequent inner criticisms, along with the grain of truth they may contain:

- **I am too much of a coward to confront ___(fill in the name of your opponent).**

Ask for details – how do I show my cowardice? Once you have heard the response, ask yourself if any of it is true, and if any is false. Deny the false parts but listen to the possibly true parts with great attention. Ask for details, until you can recognize which parts really are true. And then take a break and ask yourself why those things are true. What is the background of your so-called cowardice or reluctance to face your opponent. Perhaps you were badly hurt in the past by someone who resembles that opponent – especially if you were unable to defend yourself adequately.

As you describe the details of the true parts of your inner opponent's criticism, you will find yourself automatically seeing strategies for changing your relationship to the experience you are explaining. Either you will come to accept it – to realize that there are some situations that are simply too much for you to cope with in the moment – or to realize that you have outgrown some of the attitudes toward yourself that have fueled your reluctance to enter into conflict.

I remember one of the scariest opponents I ever went up against (at least as an adult!). It was the foreman of a machine shop in which I worked while running an engineering research laboratory in a technical university in Switzerland. At the time, foreigners were viewed with suspicion by some Swiss. My work required that I build my own apparatus in the machine shop, which inevitably caused friction between me and some of the other machinists, particularly the foreman of the shop. My work habits simply weren't up to Swiss standards. I certainly had a lot to learn from them, but I found myself being blamed for breaking tools or mistreating machines that I hadn't even touched. I became slightly paranoid, focusing more on not causing trouble than on the work at hand. And of course, this inner state led me to make errors and break tools, which I then had to report to the foreman. I became afraid of his disapproving looks and wry lectures. We were turning into genuine adversaries.

I criticized myself for being too much of a coward to confront the foreman directly. After all, I outranked him in the organization, so what did I have to lose? I had to admit that this was true. But, I told this critical voice, the foreman outranked me in other ways. My command of the language was fragile at best, and the foreman spoke no English. I knew that my command of Swiss German was especially wobbly when I was under psychological pressure. Also, he had the weight of the other machinists behind him, among whom I only numbered one real friend. And finally, I was terrified of the impersonal xenophobic hatred that smoldered all around and that threatened to singe me whenever I strayed from the path of impeccable behavior.

Realizing how much I suffered from xenophobia helped me to relax and enabled me to see the foreman both as a xenophobic Swiss—and also as a guy with troubles of his own. This perspective took the edge off my fear but still left me feeling too weak to confront him.

Which brought me to the second major inner criticism…

• **I am too weak to win a fight with ___.**

To answer this criticism you need to take a realistic and comprehensive inventory of your strengths and weaknesses. Such an inventory needs to be multidimensional—that is, to take into account not only social status (as a source of either strength or weakness) but also spiritual and psychological strength and power. In Chapters 8 and 9, I will give you a deep and thorough way to find a rock-solid basis from which to estimate your true strength and power, no matter how strong and threatening your opponent looks. But there is also a simple, quick way to find the strength to pursue a conflict for which you feel too weak. And that is to remember another situation where you did have enough strength to stand up to an opponent.

As a foreigner in that Swiss machine shop, I felt that I lacked the strength to stand up to the foreman, even though I was no longer so afraid of him. But then I remembered how I'd conducted psychological seminars at a time when I felt far too inexperienced and far less skilled than the participants I was teaching. What got me through those early seminars? My fiery enthusiasm for the subject I was teaching outweighed my lack of experience and self-confidence. And then I remembered that a similar passion guided the engineering research I was doing at the time. I felt like the lord of my laboratory, which served as a creative crucible for myself and the students who worked with, and learned from, me there. But somehow that self-assurance born of creative passion got lost on the short trip from lab to machine shop. Just remembering that energy while I was in the presence of the foreman gave me the strength to talk to him as another human being. It made me feel more like his equal and less like an adversary to be defeated.

- I am being unfair / unreasonable / bullying to ___.

Are you? Perhaps you are. But this accusation stings all the more if you are often attacked internally for being too powerful or unreasonable. Perhaps there is a good reason why you have had to come out with your anger or your guns blazing. Once you have uncovered that good reason, you will be in a better position to take the inner accusation to heart.

In short, there is almost always a grain of truth to self-accusations. But too often those self-accustions rub salt into very old wounds. At first, take that salt burn as a signal that your attitude toward old wounds may perhaps have to be updated. Once you have newly assessed those old wounds, you will probably be able to take the self-accusation to heart. Then you will be prepared for whatever the outer opponent can launch at you.

I realize now that deferring my conflict with the machine shop foreman sometimes made it hard for students in my lab to get along with me – where I was the foreman! Whatever power I lacked in my relationship to the foreman, I possessed as chief of the laboratory. I had a tendency to be extra-hard on students who acted entitled to my guidance but who disrespected and mistreated the very delicate equipment it was their privilege to use for their studies. Nowadays, when most of my hierarchical power comes from my role as a teacher, I sometimes accuse myself of being too hard on students for whom I'm responsible. And I recognize a grain of truth in this self-accusation. So when that inner accusation returns, I use it as an opportunity to re-assess my relationships with those whom I see as outranking me. But I also know that I am fair to individual students and even-handed to the groups of student with which I deal. I find, on the whole, that when I have the courage and strength to engage with those who are "above" me, my students and friends find me easier to get along with.

Accusation lies at the heart of nearly all outer, as well as inner, conflict. In the final chapter, we will explore ways of processing accusation as a major technique for befriending both outer and inner conflict.

The following exercise will guide you through concrete steps for making friends with an inner opponent, after which we will see how Janice uses it to befriend her inner version of her ex-husband.

EXERCISE:
BEFRIENDING AN INNER OPPONENT

1. **Choose a conflict** – past, present, or future – which you find yourself rehearsing in your mind.
2. **Identify the main opponent** in that drama.
3. **What bothers you the most about this person?** Make a list of your opponent's most objectionable qualities and/or actions.

4. **Are there any behaviors or qualities in your opponent that you secretly (or not so secretly) admire?** You need not ever tell the person these things – this is for your benefit only, so you can get to know your inner version of this opponent better.

5. **What does your opponent do** that overshadows his or her positive qualities?

6. **Now experiment with "shape shifting" into your opponent.** You can do this by studying how, in your imagination, your opponent walks, stands, talks, and gestures. The more details of his or hers you can try on, the more effective this exercise will be for befriending that inner opponent.

7. **As you shape-shift into your opponent, try to feel or guess into his or her view of the world** that goes along with the person's stance and behavior.

8. **As you shape-shift into that opponent, notice what aspects of his or her behavior, experience, and world view could be helpful to you, both in this conflict and in other areas of your life.** Is it the person's toughness? Sensitivity? Aggressiveness? Experiment with taking on the qualities of your opponent that, adapted to your own nature and sense of ethics, could benefit you.

9. **Now experiment with taking your new resources back into that inner conflict.** Does it change the way you interact with your inner opponent? What advice might you take with you from this experience into the actual outer conflict?

And now we'll watch as Janice goes through these steps to work on her aversion to her ex-husband.

JANICE: BEFRIENDING MY INNER "EX"

"My ex is one of the most troublesome characters in my life, even though he's almost never around. His image haunts me whenever I have trouble with my daughter. So I guess I need to work on him."

A conflict I'm constantly rehearsing? That's a no-brainer. That guy – my ex-husband – is always getting into my head. I feel we're heading toward a real confrontation, and I can't stop going over and over it in my mind.

Main opponent: That's easy. It's HIM!

What bothers me most about him is that he is smarmy. He acts happy-go-lucky, irresponsibly charming, but I feel it is all a front to get my daughter – our daughter – on his side.

Do I secretly admire something about him? You bet! It's that damned charm. I see myself as anything but charming. I'm intense, principled, responsible to a fault. And all that bastard has to do is flash that 1000-watt smile and people, our daughter in particular, get dazzled. I have to work like hell, and all he has to do is relax and turn on the charm. Boy, am I envious of him, but I'd never tell him that.

What overshadows his positive qualities? He uses his charm as a weapon against me. He uses it to make me look like an uptight creep, to get our daughter on his side whenever he and I disagree about what's good for her.

Experimenting with "shape shifting" into him: In the privacy of my own room, I first play at acting like him. At first I mimic him in a way that is meant to hurt him, but then I get intrigued. Mimicking his posture actually helps me to relax. I catch sight of myself in the mirror, slouching, smiling, relaxed, and find myself warming up to that character.

Trying on his view of life: As I play at being him, I am pleasantly surprised by the feeling of being loved by the world, without having to do anything to earn it.

How could my experience of him help me in my life? In my own skin, I feel I've got to create a social revolution before anyone will appreciate me. I feel like I work far too hard to get enjoyment out of life. If I could find a little more self-love, I think my social activism would go down a lot more easily. I'd make fewer enemies on the way to changing the world.

Taking it back to the inner conflict: When I go back to my ongoing inner dialogue with my ex, but with a little of his own self-assurance, I find I no longer have to talk down to him. I respect him more. I can argue the merits of different ways of dealing with our daughter without making him feel like an idiot. I think I could even take a bit of this attitude back to the actual outer relationship with him. I could, for instance, ask him why he has a certain approach to things, rather than just judging him to be a calculating charmer."

---

1. Thanks to Sonja Straub for pointing out this characteristic of inner criticism.

GHOST BUSTING

We've just considered some strategies for turning inner opponents into allies.

Our main tool in that endeavor was the realization that our inner opponents are part of us, even though they strongly resemble our outer opponents. To befriend our inner opponents, we need only befriend the totality of ourselves!

As we rehearse for conflict, we discover that an inner opponent is just one actor in the inner theatre of conflict. The other actors are ghosts – remembered participants in past, usually painful or destructive conflicts. Rehearsing in the inner theatre of conflict is an opportunity to "clear the decks" for effective outer conflict, by finding effective strategies to deal with the ghosts of conflict past.

The ghosts of conflict are the memories – part mental but mostly visceral – of conflicts we have seen, heard about, or been involved in. They drape their ghostly veil over the upcoming, anticipated conflict, clouding our minds, making it difficult to separate the outer reality from our remembered fears and other painful experiences of the past.

Ghosts of conflict take past situations and project them into the future. They may persuade us to avoid conflict by showing us scenes that end in defeat or damaging violence. Or they may spur us to escalate conflict by convincing us we must use all of our power to hand our opponents a ringing defeat. In either case, we may unintentionally maintain a conflict that, if we had access to greater clarity of mind, we might resolve in a way that was favorable to all.

We can tell that conflict is dominated by ghosts when we realize that we are missing the present – the here and now of relating to our opponent – and living instead in a cloudy past and threatening future. Ghosts punch a hole right through the fabric of our awareness, knocking out the "now", leaving us in a tranced-out, fuzzy, or fearful frame of mind.

These states are seldom pleasant. Many people report that they feel frozen, fearful, "not here" when in that tranced-out state. And these are the last emotions we want to feel when in the midst of outer conflict. When we are in such a cloudy, possibly fearful frame of mind, it is very difficult to care for our own interests and to avoid inflicting unnecessary pain on our opponents.

As I described in Chapter 4, the memory of my fathers angry impatience haunts me to the present day, clouding my awareness whenever I am challenged by someone who has power or authority over me. Realizing that his "ghost" is around helps me regain my clarity, enabling me to engage with the person I'm with, rather than losing myself in the memory of past conflicts with my father.

In this chapter, we will explore strategies for turning the ghosts of conflict into our allies, just as we have done in the last chapter with our inner opponents.

STALKING THE GHOSTS

When my neighbor Jerry leaned on me to give him access to his land, it woke up a whole chorus of ghosts in my inner theatre. In the blink of an eye, I was no longer talking to Jerry but remembering all sorts of situations when unreasonable (to my mind) demands had been made on me, and I had been unable to defend myself. Those remembered situations punched a hole straight through that meeting with Jerry. I could hardly hear what he was saying because I was filled with such a sense of dread. How could I possibly stick up for what I wanted when I was fighting off a whole pack of ghosts in my mind?

Who were those ghosts?

I remembered, for instance, when I was in fourth grade and Bruce Winkler, my then arch-enemy, had attacked me by pouring his soup into my already-full bowl in the school cafeteria. The hot soup overflowed, drenching my clothes. I couldn't defend myself because I was afraid of his really hurting me, even though I was just itching to get back at him!

And I remembered the unending compromises I had to make as a kid when my parents demanded things of me that I just didn't want to do — but couldn't refuse because it would:

...disturb the harmony of the family (although there was precious little of that) ... OR... disturb my parents (because they were overworked and overstressed, though I could never quite understand why) …OR… hurt my own health – although I was a really healthy kid without many problems at all.

My world as a child was full of ghosts – situations that, like hidden land mines, could blow up at any moment, but for reasons I just couldn't understand. And these ghosts all performed similar functions: they placed limits on my behavior that seemed completely unrelated to my own experience of the world. They were truly ghostlike – nearly invisible, hardly felt, yet creating a dreadful atmosphere that stayed with me into my adult life. Long after my parents were gone, their fears and prohibitions lingered just as though they'd lived on after their deaths … ghosts in the truest sense! Their influence was profound but subtle and needed only a tense atmosphere to bring it to the surface.

What sorts of atmospheres brought those ghosts back to life? All it took was a situation in which:

Someone with power over me…

- …made a demand
- …that was backed up with some sort of objective-sounding evidence
- …and the promise that peace and harmony would be restored if I would only bend to their demands.

My family ghosts did not, of course, appear in explicit form. I would not see an image of my mother with her arms crossed, a stern look on her face, outraged because I had spoiled my appetite with a slice of pizza after school. Instead, I felt a sense of unease, of instability, like I was balanced on a small perch over a yawning abyss into which I was in immediate danger of falling if I relaxed for even an instant. It is the nature of ghosts to conceal their explicit form by creating fear and uncertainty in their neighborhood.

When Jerry demanded that we give him access to his land, he had no idea of the virtual army of ghosts he awakened in me. I was knocked out of the battle nearly before it started!

BUSTING THE GHOSTS

When I was a wannabe hippy, back in the 60's (right, that's the last century, kids), "getting busted" meant that the cops found you smoking dope. You were discovered. To bust ghosts, you need to discover them in the act of their ghostly doings. And that, as in dealing with inner opponents, is at least half of the battle.

We now have some experience in dealing with inner opponents by "busting" them. We found that simply recognizing our inner chatter as a dialogue with an inner opponent was useful for reducing that opponent's power over us. This realization also opened the door to reclaiming power from that opponent, in the form of an expanded range of experience and behavior that we could profitably use in outer conflict situations. In a sense, inner opponents are a specialized kind of ghost whose effects we feel but don't really experience directly until we know what to look and listen for.

A similar strategy can help us hunt the ghosts of conflict. It is a two-step strategy. First, we can use our sense of unease to clue us to the possible presence of ghosts. And then we can apply the techniques we used to extract the value from inner opponents to make the ghosts of conflict into allies for working on outer conflict.

STEP 1: NAB THAT GHOST

"Nabbing" a ghost means catching it in the act of haunting you.

Ghosts are often shown in film and TV as a vague cloud-like vapor that "condenses" into an actual person when the hero focuses attention on it. While rehearsing for conflict, we frequently feel haunted by vague feelings, fantasies, and fears. Turning around and facing these vague feelings head-on is the first step to busting the ghosts of conflict.

Nab a ghost by fearlessly naming the vague feeling that you are having. Such feelings may include fear, rage, hatred, or, paradoxically, even happiness. These may not be feelings that you want to admit to, much less share with someone else (like your outer opponent!). But since this is an inner rehearsal, it's a great opportunity to explore feelings that might get in your way in the outer conflict.

That is how I deal with my father's ghost. When I get thick-tongued and foggy in the presence of those with power over me, just naming the experience helps get me back on track. Instead of getting lost in trying to untangle the experience, simply remembering, "Oh, that's like it was with my father," is frequently enough to break my trance. And then I can ask myself, "How would my father have dealt with this situation?" Well, I know how! He had very little tolerance for those who used social position or economic privilege to his disadvantage. Nabbing my father's ghost lets me not only regain my clarity, but also to identify how my opponent may be using his power illicitly. I can then level the playing field by tapping into my own power, rather than diminishing my opponent's, as my father would have been inclined to do.

You might name the feeling and then realize that it's not quite what you thought. That's fine. Try again. Play with facing that ghost until it begins to "condense" into something material, to take form, to develop a personality. Then you are on your way to busting that ghost by making it real and tangible.

Another way to nab a ghost is to join it in its ghostly realm. When you realize that you are being haunted by a vague feeling, let yourself embrace that vagueness instead of fighting it. As you permit yourself to let go of clarity, begin to notice any new feelings or fantasies that bubble up spontaneously. You may find that you stumble onto a new feeling that you didn't realize you had. This frequently happens when I find myself in a conflict with a friend. As in most conflicts, we get very serious as we become entrenched in our positions. Often, if I let myself relax and explore feelings and barely-formed thoughts that tickle the edges of my awareness, I find myself smiling. And then my friend smiles. That marks an opportunity to remind one another of our basic friendship, and the temporary nature of our conflict. We can then go back to the conflict with lighter hearts, knowing that whatever happens, out friend-ship will survive the stormy seas of the moment.

Or a creative fantasy might take you outside the box of an endlessly repeating inner dialogue in which you've been trapped. I once found myself slipping into a conflict while supervising a fellow therapist. He was upset with me because he felt that I had put him down in another, more public supervisory setting. Initially I tried to defend myself, then to take his side, but no matter what I did, the conflict intensified. He felt more and more misunderstood, and I grew dazed and confused, no longer certain what the actual issue was. At first, I tried to fight off the feeling of fuzzy vagueness, then when I couldn't shake it off, I decided to find out where it was trying to lead me.

I allowed myself to get even fuzzier. I seemed to fall into a kind of dream in which I was swimming around in a giant coffee cup, trying to grab hold of the rim. I thought, suddenly, "This must be significant," and decided to share the experience with my colleague. He said, "Coffee!" and smiled broadly. I asked him why he was smiling at the thought of coffee. He said, "It gives me sharp clarity, cuts through all the mist!" He became aware that, as he spoke of this clarity, he also began to feel it. And then, using the state he imagined coffee would bring him, he was able to cut through the layers of confusion to help us resolve our difficulties in a couple of minutes.

When we discussed the situation, he admitted to feeling so apprehensive at being judged by me that he simply fell into a fuzzy trance in which he gave me all the responsibility for clarifying the matter. But this didn't work, since my being clear simply made him feel more powerless and confused. Being reminded of the "coffee state" got him in touch with his own keen mind and ability to cut through the layers of fog, taking personal responsibility for clarifying things no matter what our relative power in the relationship.

This event might seem spooky, or even telepathic, but I believe it has a simpler explanation. Although fuzzy, confused states of mind may feel dysfunctional, they can be the mind's way of casting about for creative solutions to problems for which we've failed to find rational solutions. They do this in much the same way that dreams can throw new light on thorny daytime problems. Saying "yes" to fuzzy, dream-like states of mind is a way of opening ourselves to the kind of non-linear creativity that we usually see as the province of artists or poets.

STEP 2: MAKE THE GHOST CONCRETE

Although we might want to sink our ghosts of conflict in cement, what I mean here is to make them less abstract. Whether you nab the ghost by noticing its effects or by joining its world, the next step is to relate it to the here-and-now world of solid objects and thoughts.

"Busting" ghostly, indistinct feelings frequently boils them down to concrete emotions such as anger, aggression, and hurt. But we can go further, winning back even more power from them by making them more tangible.

People who act angry or aggressive may scare us because they are accidents waiting to happen. If I walk into the vicinity of an angry person, I risk having that free-floating anger directed at me. States such as anger and aggression are scary because they are not directed at anyone in particular. They are just waiting to attach themselves to anyone that comes near. Someone might pin down that angry ghost to be more specific, and then that person might say, "I'm angry at the government," or some such thing. But when we are hotter under the collar, we are, simply, "angry" or perhaps "aggressive". It exudes from us like a bad odor.

Another reason we might be afraid of people who are angry at ghosts is because we ourselves have been angry-we know what it is like to be in a bad mood that sears anyone who comes within striking distance. We can bring anger and aggression down to earth by noticing toward whom they are directed.

In my conflict with the Swiss machine shop foreman, that I recounted in Chapter 4, I used this "ghost principle" to finally resolve our difficulties. I had always felt his brooding anger toward me, but didn't understand its origin. After I got over my fear and feelings of powerlessness, I had a great conversation with him about why I broke so many tools. I explained that my father had been rather stern with me when I damaged something in our home. Now, I said, I could empathize with him, since he had grown up during the Great Depression, when possessions were hard to come by and nearly impossible to replace. As I spoke, the foreman nodded. And then, to my amazement, he smiled, and said, "Yes, I had a father like that, too." And that was the end of our difficulties. I understood that his anger had more to do with his own upbringing than with me, personally. By breaking tools, I "pushed his buttons," re-awakening an old pattern under which he silently suffered.

As soon as you notice you are getting high on anger, ask yourself exactly at what or whom you are angry. Then you can separate the wheat from the chaff. Ask yourself questions such as the following:

- Is the person I'm angry at the proper target of my anger? Or did I perhaps avoid an earlier conflict and am now getting angry at this person instead?
- To what degree am I justified in being upset with this person (or, if this is not the "real" object of my anger, with the one who is)?
- Why am I angry with this person?
- Did I avoid defending my own rights or interests at a crucial point in our interaction?
- Was I perhaps hurt by this person in a way against which I couldn't defend myself?
- Does this person have a sense of freedom, rank, or entitlement of which I am jealous? (a yes answer points to the person being a potential ally rather than just a ghostly target of my anger).

Taking stock in this way is important because it makes the ghost concrete. It transforms a diffuse and perhaps frightening mood into an opportunity to clearly consider what we are thinking and feeling-which is far preferable to getting further and further into a fogbank from which we cannot find an exit.

EXERCISE: BUSTING A GHOST OF CONFLICT

1. **Recall the conflict you worked on** in the exercise at the end of the last chapter.

2. **As you recall the conflict, take an inventory of any feelings and states of mind that come up.** Some of these may be concrete fears, such as losing a custody battle over a child, or a boundary dispute with a neighbor. But try to move beyond the immediate material fears to the vaguer, more "atmospheric" feelings that are harder to name but may tend to put you into trance-like states.

3. **As you reflect on these feelings and states of mind, try to remember any earlier experiences in which you experienced similar feelings and states of mind.** You may find that you remember only the feelings, without the concrete events. Stay with those fuzzy feelings until you remember even a little about the situation.

4. **Now try to unfold those memories of the situation more fully.** If you feel angry, try to notice at whom you're angry . If you feel afraid, of whom are you afraid? Give the emotion a face, a personality, and a context.

5. **As you go through this process, notice how it helps you separate old conflicts from the present situation.** You might gain further clarity by noticing both similarities and differences between the old conflicts and the current one.

And now, let's see how Janice works on the ghost of her own mother in her conflicts with her daughter.

JANICE: MY GHOSTLY MOTHER

"Conflict with my daughter is especially painful. I start off with a clear idea of what I want from her, but by the time we're done, I feel guilty and defeated – we seem to have a worse relationship than when we started. I feel that it's not all her fault – there's something "hanging around" that I'd like to understand better."

Recall a conflict: My daughter and I have a perennial conflict. It is like a struggle for control. Every time I make or try to enforce a rule, she finds a way to say "no," either directly or indirectly.

Feelings, states of mind, and "atmospheres": I feel like I am sleepwalking through the relationship with my daughter. Our fights have a dreamlike quality, as though time slows down like in a car accident. Although everything seems to run in slow motion, I'm powerless to stop it. I'm afraid a crisis is approaching, that she'll get hurt, or our relationship will be permanently damaged, but I can't seem to head it off.

Remember earlier experiences with similar feelings and states of mind: The atmosphere of these fights reminds me of how I felt with my own mother. I felt like I was pushing for a crisis so that I could break away from her, but at the same time felt powerless to actually provoke it.

Unfold the memories of that old experience: I remember feeling angry at my parents for the depressed mood they cast over the whole family. It was like living under a heavy fog, or a wet blanket. The only way to break free of the spell was to create a crisis in which both my and my parents' tempers flared. But the atmosphere itself made that hard to do, so when it finally happened, there was a real blow-up. As painful and destructive as that was, I still found it preferable to the smothering atmosphere of depression that permeated the household.

Separating the old conflict from the present one: As I remember back to my conflicts with my parents, but my mother in particular, I realize that I am unconsciously afraid of becoming like her. I wonder if I am becoming depressed about my life, and taking it out on my daughter by controlling her too closely. Perhaps I'm jealous of her youthful energy, not just afraid that she'll get hurt. But when I go further, and remind myself that I'm dealing with her as an inner, as well as an outer opponent, I realize that I may be selling my own youthful energy short. Could I be jealous of myself? I'm still full of idealistic fire, even if it is, in my dealings with the outer world, tempered by a strong dose of realism. I am not just depressed like my mother.

All of this makes me curious about how my daughter actually experiences me! Next time there's a fight on the horizon, I'd like to use it as an opportunity to learn more about her point of view.

WAKING UP TO POWER

Inalienable power cannot be taken from us. It is our birthright. It is the inner strength that enables us to get things done in the world. Our ability to remain in touch with this source of power is especially important before and during conflict. Waking up to our inner power is an important step toward befriending conflict.

Conflict is unpleasant in part because we stand to lose confidence in our inner power. Losing an outer conflict can shake our faith in our own power to its foundations. But even anticipating conflict can estrange us from our inner power. Attacks from our inner opponents and the ghosts of conflict can convince us to turn away from outer opponents, making it seem impossible to fulfill our own aspirations. Waking up to our inalienable power is one of the greatest challenges we face in the midst of conflict. Having access to our inalienable source of power is essential for making conflict productive and safe for both ourselves and our opponents.

How can I call power inalienable if it is possible to lose contact with it? Doesn't "inalienable" mean that it can't be taken away?

Power doesn't vanish just because we lose contact with it. It simply expresses itself in ways of which we are less aware. Power of which we're unaware can then become a liability rather than an asset.

Power expresses itself in several distinct ways even – or especially – when we do not claim it as our own. For one, it expresses itself through our body language. Even though we may feel weak, our posture, our gestures, the way we walk, and even the way we tense our muscles can all shout "power!". And because most of us have been brought up to pay attention to what we think and say, rather than to what our bodies are doing, we seldom identify with the strength our bodies are expressing.

Unclaimed power also expresses itself in our interactions with others. We do and say things to others that belie the way we see ourselves. Feeling too weak to tangle with an actual opponent, we may turn against those we see as easy targets, even though we have no real argument with them. Road rage, fits of anger at salespeople and telemarketers, and even anger at our partners and children can be our way of expressing frustration at feeling too weak to confront those with whom we have legitimate gripes. Our power is there, as its unwitting victims can testify, but we simply do not experience it as our own.

Our power expresses itself in other subtler ways. Some of us have acquired incredible strength from surviving difficult, even life-threatening, phases of our lives, particularly during our formative years. Such experiences may leave us feeling like scarred victims, but they have also toughened us against hardship. This special sort of toughness makes us into formidable opponents, even though we may never identify with the power it gives us.

Similarly, many of us have found a source of power in spiritual experience, whether through belief in a deity, through organized religious practice, or even through a relationship to nature. Spiritual experience connects us to something larger and more enduring than ourselves. We gain inner strength from that connection, and we may not realize the advantage that strength gives us in a conflict. From a psychological standpoint, we might say that we project our own inalienable power onto an outer spiritual source, or we might also experience this power as god-given and therefore outside of ourselves.

We will deal with the intricacy of these subtler sources of power in the next chapter. In this chapter, we focus on waking up to our inalienable power through relationships. We will see how simply noticing with whom we choose to engage in conflict can give us quick and lasting access to our own power, while improving our relationships at the same time.

We start off the chapter by seeing how our failure to identify with our inalienable power can lead to bullying – why, when we lose contact with our deepest source of power, we take our conflicts not to people with whom we disagree, but to those whom we can more easily overcome. This exploration will give us valuable tools for recognizing when we most need access to our inalienable power, as well as some tips on how to find it. In the following chapter, we will go deeper into the way power and our perception of its lack influence the course of conflict. There, we will practice techniques for recovering our inalienable power in situations where we feel hopelessly outranked. The self-knowledge we gain through these techniques will then help us make conflict safer for all involved, and, finally, will help us recognize and head off our tendency to become addicted to conflict.

So let's start with our tendency to take our fights to the wrong guy...

Fighting the wrong guy

There is the modern-day parable of the guy who, on a dark night, is on his hands and knees looking around on the ground under a streetlight. A friend asks, "What did you lose?"

"My keys," he says.

"Did you lose them here?"

"No, actually, I lost them on the other corner."

"So why are you looking here?"

"Because it's too dark to see over there!"

Seems absurd, doesn't it? But it may feel vaguely familiar because many of our daily conflicts are with people with whom we have no basic disagreement, but who are easier to fight with than those with whom we really have a problem!

When my computer starts acting up, I dread having to call technical support people on the phone. I feel they are either arrogant, or ignorant, or out to get me. I almost always wind up in a fight with them. And yet, who am I really fighting? I imagine that the support people are far unhappier about the situation than I am. They must speak to dozens of irate callers each day, defending products and services that they know all too well are flawed, and representing company policies that they know are meant to "handle" rather than satisfy the suckers who have already fallen for the company's sales pitch. And yet here I am once again pushing some poor guy around while feeling sorely abused by the company for which he or she works.

Despite knowing that my gripe is with the company rather than the guy I have on the line, why do I so often wind up acting like an insensitive bully, nursing a nasty joy at being able to make the poor abused fellow squirm with discomfort?

Like the guy who lost his keys on the dark corner but is searching for them on the lit corner, I know that there are real conflicts (for example, with the company that made the product) relevant to my immediate interests that I should be pursuing, but for which I lack the proper tools to go further. I am left with a sense of anger at something or someone I am unable or unwilling to address or engage to my satisfaction (we will examine the reasons for this inability or unwillingness in this chapter). And this leaves me in a rather bad mood, with a hair trigger. Other people may steer clear of me, because I look like walking trouble. I am an unfinished conflict. I'm crabby.

WHY WE GET CRABBY

All of us have gotten bitten by crabs, and I don't mean the tasty kind that live in the ocean. Crabby people seem to be looking for fights. They go around with their jaws sticking out, seeming to say, "Just hit me!"

Of course, all of us are crabby from time to time (who, me?). Why on earth do we go around looking for fights? After all, I have been repeating over and over that most of us go out of our way to avoid conflict. Am I contradicting myself? Not really. We avoid the real deal and seek out substitute opponents over which we think we have more power.

To understand why we fight with people who haven't really done much to us, we need to go back to our old friends, the inner opponent and the ghosts of conflict. When we attack someone on the outside who hasn't really done us any harm, we are placing that person into old conflicts that we've been rehearsing internally long before the outer person ever came on the scene (or on the phone).

For instance, many of us carry around longstanding conflicts with one or another of our parents – remember the ghost of my easily enraged father that I carry with me? For various reasons, we may not have been able to resolve those conflicts satisfactorily on the outside, so we continue them internally. And then, someone on the outside comes along who resembles one of those parents, and bingo! We've got somebody on whom to finish the inner fight.

If only this really worked – if we could lay those inner parents (or whomever) to rest and get on with our lives – this wouldn't be a bad strategy. And sometimes it does work. That's in part how psychotherapy works. Old Sigmund Freud, the father of psychoanalysis, understood right at the beginning that therapy was a chance for his patients to "project" their inner parents onto him so that they could duke it out in the here and now. Freud developed the theories and tools to help his patients take back their projections and to deal effectively with their inner parental figures. He also charged his patients a lot of money, which helped him bear the weight of all those negative projections they heaped on him on their way to healing.

But the people with whom we start fights on the outside as a proxy for our inner opponents – well, they aren't getting paid enough, and they usually don't have the skill or the will to deal with our fight. So they fight back, using whatever they've got. And as is usual in most unfacilitated conflicts, things escalate. Inner parents have usually been fighting us for as long as we can remember. The people on whom we project them – and then start fights with – often resemble that troublesome parent.

Rebellious teenagers who fight authority figures are often fighting an inner parental voice that tries to restrict them in ways that they find infuriating. Of course, as a teenager, you've got to internalize some of that parental voice or you'll wind up fighting everything and everyone who has the slightest bit of authority. And then you risk winding up in jail, in the hospital, or addicted to drugs. And all as ways of fighting an inner figure! At some point, you've got to turn around and confront that figure as an internal presence unless you want to wind up a rebel for life.

QUICK ON THE TRIGGER

Although some "wrong guy" conflicts come from displacing conflict from inner to outer opponents, others come from starting fights with the wrong outer opponent.

When I find myself on the attack with a telemarketer or a software-support agent, chances are the poor guy stumbled into a conflict I should have been having with someone more important in my life – my partner, one of my kids, my boss, or a colleague.

Why do we avoid conflict? The main reason is the fear that we are outranked by our opponent. I'm afraid that the other is more powerful than I am, and I will get thrashed if I start a "live" conflict.[1] I may actually be itching to "get into it," but my fear of losing keeps me from taking the plunge. And I am left with the itch that needs scratching.

Add an unsuspecting telemarketer to that energetic brew and you've got a massacre waiting to happen. Toss in anyone on the outside who (a) has less apparent power than me and (b) resembles one of the players in my internal theater of conflict, and you've got yourself a ballgame. As long as I don't have much to lose by going further, I am willing to escalate the conflict much further than I would do with my actual opponent.

My anger may seem fully justified to me, but it is significant that I feel free to exercise it on the poor guy at the other end of the phone, but not on those at whom I'm really angry.

I'm not suggesting that you give up your anger – but do notice for whom it's intended. You might get much better service from the guy at the other end of the phone and like yourself better after the call is done.

BULLYING

A bully habitually "picks on" weaker people. Most of us have experienced being bullied by bosses, acquaintances, and others who hold some sort of power over us that makes it difficult for us to react in kind.

In more reflective moments, we may wonder why a particular person who already holds most of the power needs to drive the point home so painfully to his or her underlings. Schoolyard bullies are typically the bigger, stronger kids. Don't they know they're more powerful? Why do they have to keep exercising that strength? And why not pick on someone their own size?

Though difficult to admit when we are getting beaten up, we know that the person identified as a bully in one context has been the victim of bullying in another. Having been unjustly or too-roughly handled by our boss, we are apt to come home and "take it out" on our kids. Or on the aforementioned telephone support guy. We would have loved to stand up to the bullying boss...but there wasn't enough light on that corner, so we take our suppressed visceral reactions and use them to rough up someone over whom we do have power. Bullying gets passed down the line. But no one in that line actually sees him- or herself as the bully. People who bully others see themselves as reacting to one more powerful than they. The schoolyard bully might feel abused by a parent at home, who in turn feels abused by her boss or partner.

Each and every one of us is a link in at least one chain of bullies. What better place to understand how this chain is maintained than in our own contribution to the process? If we really want to interrupt the chain of bullying, we need to find a way to throw light on the immediate conflict, no matter how intractable it may appear, rather than save up our power for a situation we are sure of winning.

We must have the courage to look up at those we fear are more powerful than us, rather than taking the easy road and looking down at those whom we feel we can easily defeat.

In addition to reducing our own tendency to bully others, a side benefit of recognizing when we are fighting with the wrong guy is that it reduces our addiction to conflict – the little tickle that makes us want to watch more and more conflict on TV, in the movies, and even in our own lives, as long as it isn't directed against us.

VITAMIN AWARENESS

For most of us the recognition that we actually bully people at some point along the way is a shock. What? I'm a bully? How awful! I've simply got to stop that kind of behavior immediately. Right?

Common sense tells us that the only way to stop doing something is to say "no" to the impulse to do it. That's a good first step. If I find myself bullying my employees, my kids, or my partner, it's probably a good idea to stop first and ask questions later. But trying to stop bullying, like so many other "bad" behaviors, is a tough assignment because the very attempt to stop it may fertilize the ground in which that behavior thrives. Trying to stop bullying others can actually make me into a bullying addict!

Like many other behaviors that we want to stop, it may first be necessary to look beneath the surface to find what makes us keep repeating it. Then, by working on its roots, it will be easier to interrupt the behavior the next time we try.

Let's see why trying to stop bullying others may make me more of a bully.

In order to stop doing something that I find harmful or objectionable, I need to first admit to myself that I'm doing it. But because bullying is despised by most people, it is almost impossible to admit to myself that I do it. By identifying myself as a bully, I am likely to berate myself for having such an awful characteristic. When I berate myself, I diminish or demolish my own sense of personal worth and power. Berating myself for being a bully is therefore a way of beating myself up—of bullying myself. But since we tend to bully others when we have been bullied ourselves, I thereby set myself up to be even more of a bully in the future! By now bullying myself about my bullying behavior, I remain trapped in the cycle of being bullied and passing it on. This is a roadmap to addiction. In Chapter 11, we will look more closely at the patterns that make bullying, and other forms of conflict, addictive. For the moment, let's see what it takes to interrupt the cycle of bullying.

Trying to interrupt destructive behavior is great if it works…but doing so without some degree of reflection is more likely to actually make the situation worse. I have learned to support my efforts to change my behavior with at least a little dose of what I call "Vitamin Awareness." A vitamin is a catalyst — a tiny bit of something that makes it easier to stay healthy. Adding even a tiny bit of Vitamin Awareness helps to interrupt that cycle by showing me that I can feel both strong and weak at the same time. And although that combination may seem impossible logically, it makes perfect emotional sense. A further benefit of Vitamin Awareness is its ability to help us understand bullying without judging (e.g., berating) ourselves. And that alone can help interrupt the vicious circle of bullying.

BULLYING CAN REMIND US OF WHO WE ARE

The first step to adding Vitamin Awareness to my behavior is to catch myself in the act — to notice that I am doing the thing that I wish to avoid. Although this step may appear to be an obvious one, staying aware of our own emotions and actions in the heat of conflict is a real challenge.

A good friend of mine described his futile attempt to stop smoking. Disgusted with his habit, he resolved to quit and threw away his pack of Parisiennes (then a popular brand in Switzerland). And then, later in the day, he suddenly found himself with a lit cigarette in his hand! He didn't know how it had gotten there! Smoking had become so ingrained in his daily behavior that he no longer had much conscious awareness of lighting, smoking, or even buying cigarettes. So noticing that he was smoking was, for him, a major event.

Instead of attacking himself for his unconscious behavior (which no doubt would have encouraged him to reach for yet another smoke), he used it as an opportunity to become aware of the mysterious power that cigarettes held over him. Rather than just turning away from the cigarettes, he turned toward them, facing them with fresh curiosity and interest, trying to decipher the awesome power that those little white sticks of shredded vegetable matter exerted over his better interests.

In the same way, we might use our own tendency to fight with the wrong guy – telemarketers, family members, our employees – to wake us up to our own strength. Nowadays, I usually identify myself as a pretty powerful guy. But at the moment I start cursing at the poor customer support agent on the other end of the telephone line, I have lost contact with that power. I am forgetting who I am and what I have accomplished. I have become (yet again) unconscious of my own effect on others, of how important my approval (or at least civil treatment) may be to those with whom I come in contact.

In the remainder of this chapter, we will examine some of the factors that lead us to start conflicts with the wrong guys – the ones with whom it's easier to win—rather than the ones with whom we really need to work out something. But my main message in this chapter is that noticing that you are fighting with the wrong guy can be the beginning of discovering new depths to your own power...and that awareness alone can help to interrupt a cycle of behavior that you've been unable to stop by brute force.

I speak from personal experience. When I was about 5 years old, I used to periodically fight with my older sister. I didn't know why I did this, especially since I got into a lot of trouble for it. My parents tried to get me to stop. I felt awful and yet got a secret satisfaction from starting fights with her. One day, after I had tangled with her once again, my father, after breaking up the fight, went out and came back with my favorite candy bar. He gave it to me without comment. That was the last time I laid a hand on my sister!

My father somehow guessed that I was bullying my sister because I didn't feel appreciated enough by him. He must have known – he had the same problem with his father! My grandfather was an educated Jew who had immigrated to America from Poland around 1905, seeking relief from abject poverty reinforced by anti-Semitism, only to find himself beset by the same troubles as in his homeland. He was a wrathful man who took out his frustration with an unjust society on his family. He was a terrible bully, all the while feeling himself a victim.

From a behavioral psychology standpoint, my father was doing precisely the wrong thing by reinforcing my destructive behavior. But he somehow knew that I fought with my sister because I felt so powerless myself. I was the victim of bullying among my friends. I wore glasses, could not catch a ball properly, and so did not participate in kids' ball games. Instead of trying to stop my behavior, my father used his awareness to guess that I felt unloved. His gesture of love despite my bad behavior cured me. Vitamin Awareness won out over punishing me for my bad behavior.

HOW DO WE KNOW?

It isn't necessary to identify with being a bully in order to know when you're taking it out on the wrong guy. For me, the most accurate measure is how I feel about what

I'm doing. No matter how satisfying it is to "go off" on someone when I'm feeling angry and frustrated, I know in my gut when I've overreacted. Some signs of an overreaction are:

- I feel bad that I got angry at someone.
- I realize that someone "pushed my buttons" – that I was sensitive or vulnerable because of past experience, and the person at whom I just got angry was only the last in a long line of offenders.
- The punishment I inflicted was far greater than the crime. Even though the other person may have been acting like a creep, he or she got a blast of anger that was way out of proportion.

STRENGTH

We pass conflict "down the line" when we do not feel strong enough to confront people and situations that put us down. As we have seen, becoming aware of when and where the bullying behavior happens is the first step toward interrupting chains of bullying that may go back several generations. But we can also do "preventive maintenance" that will give us access to the strength we need to avoid perpetuating abuse.

A first impulse might be to take stock of our own strengths and weaknesses. Simple as this step sounds, it is difficult to do for several reasons.

First, we are often unclear about how strong we really are. We tend to gauge our strength by comparing it to that of others. Our attempt to estimate our own strength is based on our prior experiences of conflict rather than on an inner sense of power. This comparative approach tends to make strength a hierarchical issue right from the start— an occasion to put ourselves down by comparing ourselves with those whom we perceive as stronger than ourselves, while at the same time supporting our sense of strength by being more powerful than others. In order to keep our sense of strength, we need to push the weaker ones further down while we attempt to pull down the stronger ones.

This view is so prevalent that many see it as the basis of natural law. We see nature as a struggle for the victory of the strong over the weak. This view of nature-as-struggle is itself the source of a great deal of conflict. Rightly or wrongly, we experience life as an endless race to get ahead of our fellow human beings or to defeat the forces of nature.[2]

I believe that this hierarchical view of strength is inevitable. It is how we become aware of who we are; it is also how we test and re-form the web of relationships that situates us in this great wide social and natural world of ours. However, if we do not look beneath the surface of hierarchical power, we risk drowning in a cycle of aggression, defeat, and revenge. But I also believe that when done with awareness, the constant testing of our own strength opens a window onto an inalienable source of power that can lift all of us up together.

In the next chapter, I will suggest a way to view and experience strength that emphasizes awareness rather than victory. This perspective will set the stage for a more general discussion of power, strength, and rank, and their contribution to conflict.

As we explore the complexities of power in the next chapter, we will gain a better comprehension of how underestimating our own power can lead us to inadvertently escalate even minor conflict. That groundwork will pave the way to the following chapter, "Practicing Safe Conflict," in which we will consider what makes conflict dangerous and what steps each of us can take to make it safer, both physically and psychologically.

Practicing safe conflict will bring us another step closer to befriending conflict as a path to improved social and personal relationships. And it will help us understand what makes conflict addictive, despite our general reluctance to get caught up in it. By understanding when and how conflict becomes addictive, we can learn how to make it more satisfying, so that we can engage in "just enough" conflict to get us where we want to go.

By going deeper into the details of strength, we will gain better tools for conducting conflict in a way that makes things better for all of us. The following exercises are provided to help you use Vitamin Awareness to connect with your own power and strength. After presenting the exercises, I will let Janice explain how she used her awareness to explore a chain of bullying in which she's involved, as well as her tendency to fight with the wrong people.

EXERCISES ON WAKING UP TO POWER

I: CHAINS OF BULLYING...

1. **Have you ever been bullied?** By whom? In what situation?
2. **How did you deal with it?** What got you through it?
3. **Were you satisfied** with the solution?
4. **Did the situation leave you with desire for revenge?** Do you ever take it out on anybody other than the original bully?

JANICE: MY LIFE AS BULLY BAIT

"Junior high school was a nightmare for me. My experiences there left me with a thirst for vengeance that's still with me."

Have you ever been bullied? I attracted bullies like honey does flies. My mother dressed me with an eye toward economy rather than style. And I had a fiery disposition, ready to go off on anyone for the slightest insult. So I was a target for two kinds of bullying—the ones who taunted me for my plain-Jane clothing, and the ones who taunted me to get a rise out of me – to see me lose my temper.

How did I deal with the bullying? I tried to outdo the bullies by doing better than them in my schoolwork. I got to be a teacher's pet by working hard. I got great grades, and that boosted my self-esteem, which lessened the sting of the bullies' taunts. In addition, the teachers liked me and gave me a measure of protection, at least in the classroom.

Was I satisfied with that solution? Not really, since it separated me from my classmates even further than I was before. And the bullies still got to me in the schoolyard, and walking to and from school, where the teachers weren't around to protect me. They would taunt me for sucking up to the teachers, and then make fun of me when I lost my cool and got furious with them.

Did these events leave me with a desire for revenge? You bet they did! I still find myself getting subtly sarcastic with anyone I feel has more social ease than I do. This really irritates my ex-husband, who is charming and gregarious. And it contributes to my jealousy of my daughter, who is popular with the kind of trendy kids from whose world I always felt excluded."

II: FIGHTING WITH THE WRONG GUY

1. **Rember a time when you had a conflict with someone who had less apparent power than you**(e.g., a shoe salesperson, an airplane steward).
2. **As you remember this experience, you may find yourself turning away from the memory** – out of shame, guilt, or just not wanting to see yourself as a bully.
3. **Now allow yourself, instead, to turn toward the memory,** but this time from a position of concern for both yourself and the person you may have bullied.
4. **What did you feel as you fought with the person?** Strength? Satisfaction? Victory? Power?

Although the fight may have been misdirected, the experiences you sought were potentially valuable. Now try taking those feelings of power and strength and imagine having access to them in a conflict with someone whom you perceive as more powerful than you, with whom you may be avoiding a conflict. Experiment with bringing those qualities into an imaginary conflict with that person. Remember to include your body feelings and movement – posture, gestures, stance – in your imaginary conflict. Does this visualization give you any hints about how to approach the pending conflict with the apparently stronger person? Does it give you the courage to pursue the conflict from a position of awareness?

JANICE: FIGHTING WITH MY DAUGHTER INSTEAD OF MY BOSS

"The vengeance I feel for my bullies in junior high still complicates my relationship with my daughter..."

Remember a conflict with someone less powerful than me: I recently had a terrible fight with my daughter. She felt I was terribly unfair when I attacked her for coming home late and apparently stoned out of her mind, after an evening out with her friends.

Turning away from the experience: I feel ashamed of how strongly I attacked her, especially since I now realize that my attack was motivated at least as much by my jealousy of her popularity as by my desire to protect her.

Turning toward the memory: As I put aside my shame and turn toward the memory, I find myself taking a more neutral view of the fight, especially in light of the work I did on the ghost of the relationship with my mother. That relationship was haunted by her mixture of jealousy of, and concern for, me. It's as if her spirit were speaking through me when I fought with my daughter. I yearn to find the right balance of freedom and safety for my daughter. And I also want to feel more secure in myself, so I don't lift myself up by putting her down.

What I felt in the conflict with my daughter: As I go further into my feelings, I realize that I enjoy feeling strong enough to get my daughter to do what I believe is right for her. I find satisfaction in being able to use my knowledge and experience to help her through a dangerous period in her life.

Experiment with another conflict where these feelings could be valuable: I'm standing on the brink of a serious confrontation with my boss. There's a kid in our care who's about to turn 18 and will be taken away from us and shifted to adult services. I know that my support of, and belief in, him have been the main things that have kept him in school and out of trouble, despite several changes of foster homes. I've been avoiding a showdown with my boss on this issue, since I know the rules are all on his side, and I lack the clout to get my way. But now I feel sobered by my experience with my daughter. I'm afraid that if I don't stick to my guns by standing up for what I know is right for this kid, I'll let him down, and I'll probably go back to fighting with my daughter – trying to do for her what I couldn't do for him. And I'm also afraid that this would irritate my relationship with my ex even further, because I know I really can exercise power over him. So I know now that I've got to get into the fray with my boss, no matter what the outcome."

---

1. There are, of course, lots of other possible reasons. For instance, I don't want to hurt the other person. But as we will see shortly, the notion that I don't want to hurt my opponent contains the idea of *wanting* to hurt him or her and rejecting the possibility – for any of a variety of possible reasons. Whenever I hear someone say, "I don't want to hurt you," I prepare to get hurt!

2. Although this viewpoint is often attributed to Charles Darwin, his motto "survival of the fittest" did not mean "survival of the strongest" but survival of the species that could reproduce most efficiently – the *reproductively* fittest.

Rank, Role, and Inalienable Power

We finished the last chapter with a first look at the role strength plays in conflict – how underestimating our own strength can inadvertently lead us to fight with those we can overpower, rather than those with whom we have legitimate disagreements. We concluded that when we become aware of our tendency to take it out on the wrong guy, we are on the threshold of waking up to our own inalienable source of power – a source that will never abandon us, even in the midst of the most difficult conflict.

Bullying and abuse are not the only hazards of being unaware of our power. Escalation is fueled by each side underestimating its own power. When we feel weak but are not aware that we are acting strong, conflict can spiral out of control, beyond the intent of either opponent, until someone gets hurt or the conflict becomes entrenched. War, feuds, and vendettas are the result of escalating conflict, like a major forest fire developing out of a spark from a campfire or a discarded cigarette.

The problem with judging our strength by comparing ourselves to others is that we are likely to start escalating conflicts by the very process of comparison. When kids "horse around" with each other, their little skirmishes that begin good-naturedly can get out of hand and turn into a real fight if they lose sight of their initial playfulness and focus too much on winning.

We therefore need to find sources of inner strength that don't depend on how strong we think our opponents are. When we are in touch with these inner resources that cannot be taken from us, our opponents' apparent strength is no longer so hypnotic. We are freer to choose how much of our strength we bring to bear on the outer situation. We will find that this not only makes conflict safer, it also reduces the addictive quality of conflict. We can bring conflict to a definitive conclusion more quickly, instead of coming back to the same issues time and time again.

STRENGTH AND POWER

The conventional way of measuring strength is quite simple. We compare our physical strength with that of someone else. Who can lift the heaviest weight? Who can run faster? Farther? Who can win a wrestling match?

But when we leave the gym or playing field, power – the ability to get things done – is not so simple to measure. It is not just force against force, strength against strength. For the purposes of the following discussion, we'll use the word strength to refer to the ability to do more or less of something, compared to someone else. We'll reserve power for something more complex – the ability to use all of one's strengths to actually get things done in the world. Let's look at a couple of familiar scenarios to see some of the differences between strength and power.

WHO'S GOT THE POWER?

I sometimes find myself getting annoyed with children in situations where I just can't get away from them. It brings me to the edge of conflict. But is it really possible for an adult to have a useful conflict with a child? After all, kids are so weak, and I'm so big and strong by comparison. Nevertheless, sometimes things get out of hand...

I spend a lot of time in airplanes, since my work takes me to Europe several times a year. If I am lucky, I get a seat to myself so I can spread out and catch some sleep. But now and again, just as I am settling down, I feel a little kick through the back of my seat. A young child is idly swinging his (it's often a boy) leg, rhythmically kicking me through the seatback.

This immediately creates a mini-crisis inside of me. How should I handle the situation, since the child and I will be in close contact for the next nine hours? I have learned that it is better to say something friendly but assertive to the child and his parents right off the bat, before I've built up a head of steam. But after that, I am on guard, because things seldom end there. And the next kick I feel, I get angry. Why aren't the parents controlling their child better? I know why – it can be a daunting project bringing kids on a long plane trip, stressful for both them and the parents. But I've paid a lot of money for that seat, and I feel that I deserve some peace and quiet.

If I just get furious with the kid, I come across as a bully. After all, I am the big, strong guy, and the kid is just

– a kid! I'm more powerful, right? Of course, the situation is far more complex than just who's bigger and stronger.

First off, kids are powerful. They can create large disturbances despite their small size and physically weaker bodies. That kick, those lungs when they start to cry – there's nothing weak about them. Also, they derive power from being kids. Kids are (at least in theory) protected from adult strength through law and often through custom. I've heard of parents being put off a flight for being a little rough (in someone else's eyes) with their kids. Furthermore, kids really know how to provoke adults. I remember getting an enormous amount of satisfaction from "getting a rise" from my father. Kids know how to use their power to stir up trouble!

Secondly, the child is backed up by his parents' strength. Even though he might not be able to stand up to me, his parents are likely to spring to his defense, getting upset with me because I have dared to criticize their darling's behavior (even though, at another time, they may get upset by precisely the behavior that is annoying me!).

In many ways, the kid has the upper hand! And it has happened that, despite my knowledge of power and its subtleties, I've had to endure getting kicked all across the Atlantic Ocean and well into Eastern Europe.

Even this commonplace situation shows that it's impossible to rank one person's power against another's on a simple scale. Strength has many dimensions that combine in complicated, interesting, and sometimes maddening ways. All of these dimensions add up to power – the ultimate ability to get something done, or prevent someone else from doing it.

Besides physical strength, what are some of the other dimensions of power? Let's go to that ancient manual of powerful beings, the Bible, for our next insight.

DAVID VS. GOLIATH: VICTORY AGAINST ALL ODDS

Many of us – especially if we were brought up in the Judeo–Christian tradition – were inspired by the Biblical tale of David and Goliath. There's Goliath – a great giant of a man, a heartless and single-minded warrior, about to reduce David to a grease spot in the desert. And there's David – smaller and weaker than Goliath, but with justice on his side. He kills the giant with a single stone from his simple sling shot.

We are drawn to this tale because it challenges the dismal apparent inevitability of the strong trampling the weak. Even if we are smaller or weaker than our opponent, there are other factors – like the justice of our position or our relationship to God, spirit, or the universe – that could help us prevail against the odds.

The story of David and Goliath highlights a complex relationship of power to conflict that goes against our fixed idea that the strong will defeat the weak. It makes us think twice about the role of physical strength in conflict. Most of us identify more with David than with Goliath. Is it possible that we could really win conflicts despite feeling weak and puny beside our opponents?

Our common sense screams "NO!" The race belongs to the bigger, faster, and stronger. But David's victory tells us, "Maybe yes, maybe no!" Perhaps power is more than skin (or muscle) deep.

What advantages did David have over Goliath that helped him defeat the giant? The tale suggests that he had God on his side – on the side of the just, rather than the merely strong. Whether or not "God" actually exists – and that's not something we're going to get into here – the belief in God – any god – is a source of strength that many of us recognize as being at least as powerful as physical strength. We know from firsthand experience that when we relate to something greater than ourselves – be it a deity, nation, or an ethnic, racial, or gender identity – we feel more powerful than when we stand alone against a strong opponent.

Relative strength in conflict

We think and speak about conflict in terms that come from athletic contests and war, two areas of activity where strength and power are the most obvious resources for victory.

For instance, in my conflict with Jerry over property boundaries, I found myself SIZING HIM UP (what you do in a fist fight, when you are seeing if your opponent is bigger, and likely stronger, than you). I thought of him as a TOUGH GUY (a bruiser, someone who could go a few rounds in a fight), because he had the persistence and physical stamina to survey the steep hillside property single handedly. I also found myself colluding with both my partner Kate and my next-door neighbors to forge a unified FRONT (an expression from warfare), because I didn't feel strong enough to confront him alone on the issues. And always, I was comparing myself to him. Who was the stronger in his ability to convince, or even intimidate, the other into believing that he was right?

I did not do this consciously, like by asking myself, "Which one of us will win if things get down and dirty?" It was rather an ongoing, almost automatic appraisal and re-appraisal, JOCKEYING for position, finding little CHINKS IN HIS ARMOR, finding and nurturing ALLIES.

Comparing my strength to my opponent's is a good precaution. I don't want any unpleasant surprises when we finally move into the arena. But it's difficult to know my own strength. Because we are dealing with inner opposition as well as ghosts of conflict past and future, we tend to underestimate our own strength. We forget that we are consuming a lot of power by fighting these inner battles. And for that reason we tend to come out swinging harder than we really intend to. Put that together with a similar tendency on the opponent's side, and we get a dangerous situation. Two people, each of whom feels weaker than the other, set about mustering all the force they can. And the harder each fights, the weaker the other feels! It is an unstable situation. It is escalation.

If we want to practice safe conflict, with the goal of improving rather than destroying our relationships with one another, we need to find a reliable way of valuing our own strength, regardless of how strong or weak our opponents may appear.

STRENGTH AND RANK

Physical strength, like a person's height or weight, is measured on a scale, from a little to a lot. It takes very little strength to lift a feather and quite a lot to lift a boulder. We "rank" one another similarly, on scales of importance, strength, or power in society and in organizations.

When it comes to conflict, it may be a matter of life and death to correctly estimate the strength of my opponent. Estimating my opponent's strength is complicated by the fact that physical strength, as we have seen, is not the only factor that decides who wins and who loses, nor is it sufficient for predicting whether conflict will be safe or dangerous. Both my story of the child kicking my airline seat and of David beating Goliath show that ultimate power in a conflict is not just a simple comparison of the physical strength of the two opponents. We need to be able to get a rapid estimate of both our own and our opponent's total strength – all the resources that we, and our opponent, have at our disposal, and how those resources are likely to be used if we should actually engage in conflict.

Recent world events have shown us just how complex estimating the power of opponents can be. The United States, for instance, has long regarded itself as being superior in physical strength, as measured by the number, destructive capability, and accuracy of its weapons. And yet, in recent history, the USA has been held at bay, if not defeated, by groups and nations who, on conventional scales of power, are far weaker than itself. It appears that ranking the strength of nations by the size and strength of their armies is not a reliable indicator of who will win an armed conflict! But this fact runs so strongly against our conventional wisdom that we fall, time and time again, into the trap of thinking that physical power is all that is needed to win conflicts. We need a more accurate way of ranking the strength of opponents in order to predict the outcome of a conflict.

UNDERSTANDING POWER

What goes into estimating someone's total power, both in everyday life and in conflict? What makes it more likely that one person, rather than another, will be able to get his or her way?

First of all, there are factors that determine our position in a hierarchy, or our rank, with regard to one another. Physical strength, size, and weight clearly play a role in determining our rank.

Social factors also play an important part. There are privileges —mostly unearned – that go along with aspects of our social identities and play a decisive role in our ability to win in conflicts. Gender, age, sexual orientation, education, and wealth all play a significant part in determining our social rank or power in comparison to others. Some of these factors have to do with our position in an organization. The boss outranks his or her secretary, who outranks the guy who distributes the mail, who outranks the night watchman. When it comes to a conflict in the office, those who are occupy higher positions in the hierarchy have more leverage and are more likely to win.

Then there are subtler factors that depend more on our experience of ourselves and others than on outer structures or physical strength. When used comparatively, they are called psychological and spiritual rank. I will describe these in more detail in the following section.

And finally, there is power related to our values. Our chances of winning a conflict are related to how far we are willing to go in order to get our way. Many of us have had the experience of "letting off the brakes," of "letting fly" with our emotions, or of "losing it" and attacking someone else with almost superhuman strength we didn't know we had.

When any of these sources of power are used unconsciously, they can be anywhere from extremely irritating to our opponents to downright dangerous. And we are most likely to use them unconsciously when we are not in touch with them, when we identify only with our most superficial sources of strength.

Unconscious use of power makes conflict unsafe because we don't see how it affects our opponents. If we did, we would instantly see how powerful we actually are, regardless of how we experience ourselves internally. Just as we used Vitamin Awareness to wake us up to our power when bullying someone weaker than we, we can learn to make better use of power that we've used unconsciously up to now.

Next let's now take a look at some of the subtler factors that contribute to power – both conscious and unconscious — before we consider how our bottom-line values affect the way we engage in conflict.

BEYOND PHYSICAL STRENGTH: PSYCHOLOGICAL TOUGHNESS AND THE SPIRITUAL CONNECTION

Looking beyond physical strength to subtler aspects of our power has at least two potential benefits. First, we will begin to recognize aspects of our own strength with which we do not yet identify, but which are clearly visible to others, particularly those with whom we have potential conflicts. And second, we will become more aware of these sources of power in others, especially those potential opponents who do not appear at first glance to be particularly powerful or threatening.

These subtler strengths are often easier to see in others than in ourselves. I experience my neighbor Jerry as a tough and stubborn negotiator but fail to see the same qualities in myself. I may be overwhelmed by a powerfully charismatic speaker who leaves me lost and mumbling like a fool.

Toughness implies tough-mindedness – someone who does not easily give up his or her position, even when under great pressure to do so. Toughness comes from experience – from an education in the school of hard knocks. Those of us who have had to defend ourselves against physical attack and psychological abuse – particularly in our childhood – and have survived the process, gain intimate knowledge of our own strengths, weaknesses, and abilities. We are less willing to take on others' views of our strengths. We become harder to intimidate. We acquire a power that Arnold Mindell has termed "psychological rank."

Charisma refers to the ability to captivate another, to weave a sort of spell or charm that puts the charismatic person at the center of the proceedings. Although physical power may contribute to charisma, it is more an attitude that is expressed through the charismatic person's posture, gestures, speech, and a way of relating that makes you feel, even in a crowded room, that he or she is talking directly and intimately to you and you alone.

Charismatic people seem to derive their power from a transpersonal source. They represent not themselves but a spiritual principle. Remember David's defeat of Goliath? That defeat gave him enough charisma to guarantee him a feature role in the Bible itself. He became a king. The power we gain by identifying with transpersonal principles is what Arnold Mindell has called "spiritual rank."

Both of these sources of power – psychological and spiritual rank – usually escape our awareness when we are sizing up an opponent. And yet, we feel the effects of these sources of power, even if we don't recognize them directly.

In my confrontation with my neighbor Jerry, I felt exhausted and outranked by his toughness. I felt that no matter how much I argued with him or threatened him, he could coolly outlast my tirades.

IDENTIFYING WITH POWER

Like any source of power, spiritual and psychological rank are easier to react to in others than to recognize in oneself. And just as in the case of unclaimed physical strength, spiritual and psychological rank that I don't recognize or own in myself becomes a provocative irritant in relationships in general, and conflict in particular.

I was trained as a psychotherapist, as was, fortunately, my partner Kate. I say fortunately because we are both alert to the potential abuse of spiritual rank that can be a side effect of therapeutic training. It is sorely tempting, in the midst of an argument, to take the spiritual high ground by "understanding" my opponent's position rather than addressing her actual complaints. When it is too painful to consider the possible truth of the other person's accusation, I can retreat to my "superior" view of her psychological and spiritual motivations and put everything back on her, much to the detriment of our relationship. So great is the temptation of "psychologizing" one another that Kate and I have an explicit rule of "no psychology" when we are having an argument. Afterwards, each of us is free to psychologize ourselves, but we have learned that using spiritual rank to win an argument is neither fair, satisfying, nor sustainable.

Notice that I call the power I acquire from my psychological training spiritual, not psychological, rank. That's because the power comes from relating to something larger than my own ego. I am trained to search for the person's wholeness —his or her unconscious as well as conscious experience and behavior – which gives me access to something larger and deeper than the normal social plane of relationship: what some would call the spirit or the soul. And that is the definition of spiritual rank: power and privilege that come from a relationship to something larger than one's own identity.

Psychological rank can also be abused, though in a somewhat different way. In its most irritating form, psychological rank is intimately connected to a feeling of victimhood. Someone (in a way, each of us) who has survived ongoing painful, abusive, even life-threatening treatment at some point in his or her life is faced with a difficult choice. Should the person identify with his or her victimization and seek compensation for the pain? Or should the person identify with the power that endured the agonizing experience and that now allows him or her to participate in the present world?

Suppressing the agony of a hard life is not healthy. By denying our pain, we set ourselves up for future, possibly ongoing, abuse. But suppressing the strength that got us through those experiences is equally hazardous, particularly combined with a strong sense of victimhood and a thirst for vengeance.

In my youth, I and my friends were scared of "those" kids, the tough ones with slicked-back hair, narrow pants, and leather jackets. In those days they were called "juvenile delinquents." Many of them came from underprivileged and abusive homes, but we didn't know that. They scorned authority, harassed teachers, tormented kids like me, and made a generally obnoxious and dangerous impression. I didn't now anything about their backgrounds. Coming from a relatively loving and highly supportive home (punctuated by occasional outbursts by my parents, when they were pushed to their limits), I had no experience of parental abuse (at least, not overt abuse, in the way that these kids experienced from their parents). So all I saw was their strength, not the sense of impotence to which they were reacting.

And to think that despite this image of myself, I, too, had a reputation for being powerful in ways with which I didn't identify! I, too, had unclaimed psychological rank. Mine took the form of uncontrollable rages. Although I usually identified myself as a victim of the school's bullies, I could give as good as I got. I just didn't see it as aggression. I saw it as the last resort of a poor victim pushed up against the end of his world. When pushed too far, I could fight, and I fought dirty. My language lit up the air with colors unknown to most of my classmates – language that I'd learned from my father, when he was in one of his rages.

My process of waking up to my own power has required that I recognize and own my psychological rank – the feisty toughness that got me through a childhood of marginality and bullying—because I know that when I identify only with my victimhood, I become dangerous to myself and others.

To put the point more strongly, the person who identifies only with his or her victimhood is, in the end, ripe for a career as a terrorist. For the person who feels that he or she has lost everything to others, nothing remains but vengeance. And this brings us to another dimension of conflict that is intimately connected with our sense of strength and weakness: Just how far are we willing to go to win a conflict?

ULTIMATE POWER

In most cases, the stronger party can win a conflict if winning is the only goal. During the Cold War, certain American military leaders wanted to launch a nuclear strike against the Soviet Union to prevent the Russians from attacking us. They thought that nuclear war was inevitable and that we'd better deliver the first blow while the Russian arsenal was still weaker than ours, or else risk total annihilation when the Russians caught up with us in the "arms race."

Bringing all of one's strength to bear on a conflict is a desperate move. Given the risk that the opponent may have unseen reserves or the ability to build powerful coalitions, it is a go-for-broke strategy that can as easily result in total destruction of both sides, as it can a victory for one.

We are all familiar with this idea on a much smaller scale in interpersonal conflict. We usually retain enough awareness, even in the nastiest of fights, to stop short of annihilating our opponent. Awareness of what? Of our goals – the "bottom line" of what we are actually hoping and trying to achieve through conflict, as well as the possible cost of victory.

In the first chapter of this book, I told of two conflicts in which I was engaged. I "won" both, but my criteria for winning and losing were very different in the two cases.

In the first, I grew enraged at a hotel desk clerk for what I saw as the management's mistreatment of me. When the clerk was unresponsive, I reached across the desk and tore up the credit card slip I had just signed. I had won but felt bad about my victory. I had gone for broke, using all of the power I had available to defeat my "opponent." Never mind that my real opponent was the hotel business itself. The clerk, low-paid flack-catcher for an uncaring management, was simply the easiest target for my wrath. I was being a bully, attacking not the one with whom I had the real conflict, but the one who was most accessible and easiest to overpower.

My bottom line in that case was winning, no matter what. That freed me to use all of my power, regardless of the effect it had on others. By choosing a target with greater restraint than I had, I ensured my victory. If the clerk had been less restrained, we might have wound up in a physical fight, or I might have been thrown out of the hotel by someone bigger and stronger than I.

In the second conflict, I was trying to get an airline ticket agent to get me on his airline's flight because I'd missed the last flight on another airline. I knew it was possible for him to do this, and I felt that his reluctance was mere bureaucratic inertia. I felt that if I merely overpowered him, he would use his authority to deny me the ticket, and I would once more feel like a bully. My final tactic was to put him in touch with his own power – which I guessed to be greater than that with which he identified! Both of my goals were satisfied. He got me the tickets, and he discovered a new power that he hadn't realized was his!

RANK AND ROLE

What these stories have in common is the importance of power and hierarchy in instigating as well as resolving the conflicts. In both of these cases, my opponents were stronger than I within the framework of their jobs. The hotel clerk wrote my bill and took my credit card. The power to accept or refuse my arguments ultimately lay with her. The airline ticket agent wore a uniform, sat behind the airline counter, and had control over who did or didn't get tickets.

I knew nothing about either of these people as individuals. But each had power over me by virtue of their roles in the businesses for which they worked.

The hotel clerk may, for instance, have been under the thumb of an oppressive mother – in her role as a daughter, she would have little power. Or (and!) she might have been a black-belt Karate instructor when she got off work at the hotel — wielding awesome physical and psychological power over her students.

I never had a chance to learn anything about her as an individual, because I reacted to her as though she were identical with her hotel-clerk role. Within the framework of the hotel business, she outranked me. In today's business world, the customer holds little power compared to the management. As businesses grow larger and less personal, they need only satisfy their customers on a statistical basis; the satisfaction of the individual grows ever less important. The corner grocery store owner needed every customer he or she could get, because the competitor on the other corner needed customers, too. And since those customers lived around the corner, the grocer had to be careful about who he or she antagonized.

But since my bottom line was WINNING, I felt free to counter the hotel clerk's higher structural rank with the sheer power of my anger and the loudness of my voice. Feeling weak, I dug into my reserves and brought out all of my strength – short of physically assaulting her! I thank her to this day for her restraint. If she had participated in my escalation strategy, I might have started my day with a run-in with the police.

Things went differently with the airline agent because my goals had shifted by then. Although he outranked me by virtue of his position in the airline, I also saw him as an individual trying to fill a difficult role. This awareness freed me to pay attention to what he was saying rather than just try to overcome his power. At first I tried the tactic of taking his side by trying to feel my way into his position. But when he still refused to give us the ticket, I grew angry. I thought he was merely standing behind the power of his role after I had reached out to him personally, trying to understand why he couldn't meet my request.

At this point, I might have thrown good intentions to the winds and escalated the argument, as I felt he had done by ignoring my attempt to understand his position. But I realized that although escalation might satisfy my need to come out on top, it would neither get me my ticket nor make either of us happier in the long run. I would once again have fought with the wrong guy – bullied him – and gotten only the shortest "fix" from feeling momentarily righteous.[2]

EYES ON THE GOAL

Because my larger goal included maximizing both the ticket agent's and my happiness, I could not simply increase the pressure until the argument turned into a fight. So my alternative was to pay closer attention to the details of our interaction. I noticed immediately that he did not say "I won't do it," but "I can't do it!" Despite the fact that he, not I, held the power, he felt insufficiently strong to take the ticket exchange into his own hands. He was looking up, toward his bosses, in the hierarchy of the moment, rather than down, to me, the poor, suffering customer. As soon as I realized this, I decided to appeal to a deeper, more personal side of both of us by challenging him, strongly and directly, to step into his own personal power. By saying (cringe!) "Your balls are bigger than you think they are," I was using powerful language to address a more primal layer of his experience of himself. And he rose to the challenge by taking on a new degree of authority. He changed roles within what must have seemed to him like a fixed, dreary hierarchical system in which he had little freedom to express his own power and initiative.

WIDENING THE PERSPECTIVE ON POWER

We often view our rank in hierarchical systems from much too narrow a perspective. We tend to underestimate our own power by comparing it to those above us, whom we imagine to be more powerful, rather than to those who occupy less powerful roles. We identify with the power connected to the role we play in a particular situation, forgetting the totality of our outer and inner resources.

As my encounter with the ticket agent shows, power can shift in the blink of an eye. We can do things that only a moment before, we felt were impossible.

And finally, we forget that our greatest strength, our deepest power, comes not from our position in a hierarchy but from our own relationship to ourselves, the world, and spirit. Whereas rank – the power we garner by comparing ourselves to others – can shift like water or sand, the deeper power of self-knowledge is ours for the keeping. It can never be taken from us.

INALIENABLE POWER

This all seems like a lot to remember when we're preparing for friendly conflict – it sounds like you'd need to take a whole course to get all the details straight. That is because rank – comparative power – has many dimensions and is communicated in many ways, some of them quite subtle. If your job is to facilitate others' conflicts, it pays to learn about the details of rank.[3]

Fortunately, there is a shorter path to the same goal. You can go a long way to bypassing the whole rank issue by staying in touch with your own inalienable power – that source of inner strength that is yours alone. It is not dependent on the strength of others around you. It is a resource that is yours whether you're confronting your own David or your own Goliath.

Each of us has our own unique way of getting and staying in touch with our inalienable power. Some of us do it by reflecting on who we are and what we have accomplished in the world. The great psychiatrist Carl G. Jung went through a period in his life when he feared he might be going crazy. He was seeing things and hearing voices that were growing increasingly disturbing to him. At moments when he thought he was losing touch with reality, he would go into his study and look at his medical school diploma hanging on the wall and think, "I am C. G. Jung, I have a medical degree from the University of Basel, I own a house, I am married and have children. I can't be that crazy!"

Our bodies are another reliable source of inalienable power, even when we feel physically weak or ill. You might try, as you are reading this, relaxing, letting yourself feel what is happening in your body, than asking yourself, "Where is the source of power in my body?" Wait until you feel that power somewhere in your body. It may be tempting to fantasize, imagine, or visualize where that power is. But have patience and allow yourself to really feel it. The more your sense of power is anchored in a body feeling, the more reliable it will be and the less subject to influence by others.

Once you have found that source of power in your body, try making a little dance that expresses the feeling. It could be a very little dance, like just a subtle movement of your fingers or a hand. Or it could be a short movement that involves more of your body. Again, don't invent too much or embellish it — try to stick close to a movement that expresses the original feeling, that helps you go back to that feeling quickly and reliably.

Still others find their inalienable power with the help of a teacher, a spiritual guide, or some other role model. If just one person whom you love or respect has faith in your inalienable power, it may be possible to gain access to that power by remembering that person's faith in you.

Many of the leaders we most admire – Gandhi, Martin Luther King, Jr., and Nelson Mandela, to name but a few – were able to produce sweeping social change not by violent revolution but by putting people of low social rank in touch with their own inalienable power. These leaders empowered people not by giving them power but by putting them in touch with their inalienable power. Power that is given can also be taken back. Power that we discover in ourselves is ours forever.

Gandhi did empower others in part by joining the people he was trying to free from British rule. He adopted a simple lifestyle, walking instead of riding, spinning cotton, dressing simply. He paid special attention to those with the lowest social rank – the Dalits or untouchables – because he knew that the caste system was one of the main obstacles to freeing the Indian people from oppression. He called them "children of God" to underscore his belief that all of us come from, and derive our most important powers from, fundamentally the same source.

Martin Luther King placed emphasis on the power of dreaming – of believing in a reality other than the one dictated to us by our social and economic oppressors. In his famous "I have a dream" speech, King put forth a vision of racial equality that seemed totally unrealistic by the standard of that day's social reality. But by asking others to dream with him, King gave us all access to a world that transcends realities that are incomplete because they have been determined by less than the totality of humankind. A reality that is determined by only the highest ranking stakeholders in a society marginalizes the power that is available to all of us. Believing in that reality deprives us all of self-esteem, of the belief that we can ever be part of the mainstream that participates in the definition of reality itself.

Nelson Mandela placed great emphasis on the right to education – and the belief that all of us are equally capable of being educated. He believed – and transmitted this belief to the peoples of South Africa – that we can all unfold our true potential, and that to do so is part of our birthright.

Getting in touch with your inalienable power is easy. Staying in touch with it in the face of conflict is difficult. That is why it pays to come back again and again to the experiences and relationships that support your sense of inalienable power – to practice reaching for it in the moments when you feel the least powerful, the most outranked by others. Because if you can connect with that source of power, it will make you a much safer and helpful opponent. Conflict will not seem as daunting, because when you are in touch with your inalienable power, there is really very little that you can lose. A reliable connection to your inalienable power will serve you better than all the property and companionship in the world. For when the chips are down, you will still have yourself.

In the next chapter, we will explore how adding Vitamin Awareness to our understanding of rank and roles can make conflict safer. Safety is a significant part of our goal of befriending conflict so that it lives up to its full potential to bring us closer together, rather than drive us apart.

The following exercise will help you get in touch with a source of inalienable power and experiment with referring to it in an upcoming conflict. After that, we will look in on Janice as she searches for a source of inalienable power to use in the upcoming conflict with her boss.

EXERCISE: FINDING A SOURCE OF INALIENABLE POWER

1. **Remember a situation in which you felt you had sufficient power.** It might have been a conflict, or it might have been a situation in which you felt satisfied and capable, despite the presence of others who had more apparent power than you did.

2. **Allow yourself to go back to that situation. Remember how you felt.** Try standing or sitting the way you did in that situation. Try speaking and moving the way you did in that situation. Notice the effect on your mood; on the feelings in your body.

3. **Make a small movement that will help you "anchor" this mood, feelings, and attitude.** It could be just a tiny movement of one finger, but make sure it expresses something of that power you experienced in the previous step.

4. **Make a drawing that expresses that power.** Again, it could be a single line, as long as it reminds you of that power.

5. **Now remember a situation in which you felt you had insufficient power.** Briefly visit the feelings, thoughts,

and your way of speaking and moving in that situation. Don't dwell on these, or you might get stuck feeling awful!

6. **As you remember the situation in which you felt insufficiently powerful, make the power movement of Step 3.** Perhaps it would also help to make a drawing, as in Step 4, that expresses your power.

7. **Notice the effect this has on your feelings,** as you remember the situation in which you had insufficient power.

8. **How might you use this experience to prepare for an upcoming conflict,** particularly one in which you are afraid of being overpowered?

JANICE: CONNECTING WITH MY INALIENABLE POWER

"I am at my powerful best working with some of the most challenging kids that our agency cares for. I'd like to use the power and assurance I have in those situations in my relationship with my boss, which I feel is often strained by the power he has over me, and the way I react to his power..."

I remember a situation in which I was satisfied with my power: I was able to relate to and motivate a seemingly intractable young man who had been passed on to me by a co-worker who felt helpless and intimidated by him. I recognized and respected his intelligence, and at the same time was able to challenge his tough and disrespectful style of relationship. Under my guidance, he was able to finish high school and go on to community college.

How the situation felt to me: I remember meeting him for the first time. I recognized a bit of myself in him. I felt myself leaning back with a kind of "I rule the world" entitlement that I got from having survived my depressed home and the bullying of my classmates. I noticed – and was proud of – how different I seemed from the rigid, somewhat frightened-looking case worker who had referred him to me. As I ease into that memory, I can feel the strength of my own rebellious youth flowing back into my body. I feel a subtle thrill at the feeling that I could stand up to anyone, no matter how much power they wield over me.

Anchoring the power experience: As I remember the situation with the young guy, I notice myself leaning back in my chair. I feel the flexibility and strength of the long muscles of my back and limbs.

Sketching the power experience: I'm not a good artist, so I draw a single arc on a piece of paper. It looks to me like a bow that is only slightly bent, but could store and release an enormous amount of power if needed.

Briefly revisit a situation in which I felt insufficiently powerful: I remember past confrontations with my boss in which I've felt overpowered by him. I've usually tried to placate him, speaking softly and escaping from his office as fast as possible.

Bringing the power experience of step 3 to this conflict: I go back to the upcoming confrontation, but this time I try stretching and relaxing at the same time, like a bow ready to be bent and release an arrow at a moment's notice.

Noticing how this affects my feelings as I imagine the upcoming situation: When I focus on that bow-like experience in my muscles, I notice that I feel more comfortable in my boss's presence. I feel more relaxed, surer of my strength, even though the power of his position and the organization are on his side.

How this could prepare me for an upcoming conflict: I'm still thinking about the upcoming confrontation with my boss that I mentioned in the exercise in the last chapter, where I want to fight for the rights of an endangered kid. In the past, my sense of impotence in my boss's presence kept me from discussing crucial issues with him. I came to see him as an absolute authority, and therefore an enemy to be conquered, rather than as a potential ally in getting the best treatment for our clients. Now, as I feel that strength in my body, I begin to see him more as a person and less as a power to be defeated. I wonder if he, too, might have been as idealistic as I was when he first took his job. Perhaps I could motivate his old sense of idealism to help me solve the problem, rather than simply following the rules.

---

1. Interesting enough, in today's hyper-impersonal world of Internet shopping, attention to the individual customer's needs is becoming once more important at neighborhood stores. This has resulted in extremely liberal return policies on everything from clothing to electronics.

2. This is a preview of how conflict becomes addictive!

3. See, for example, Mindell's *Sitting in the Fire*, and Fuller's *Somebodies and Nobodies*.

PRACTICING SAFE CONFLICT

A prime reason for avoiding conflict is that it can be dangerous. Say the "C" word and people cringe – they imagine things getting out of hand and turning violent. But if we look at the range of conflicts in which we are involved in our daily lives, we realize that only the smallest number of them (if any) ever turn physical.

Violence can be psychological as well as physical. We hurt each other with language – sharp words, tongue-lashings, and verbal abuse are all familiar aspects of spoken conflict. Sarcastic remarks are a form of psychological violence because they are intended to hurt. And we hurt each other with our moods by creating intolerable emotional atmospheres that punish by their bleak persistence.

Conflict need not be hurtful. There are many things like conflict that are actually fun, even though they can be quite dangerous both physically and emotionally. Athletic and other competitions, games, debates, political arguments – all of these skate close to conflict and sometimes cross the line. But there is a difference in intent and goals that makes them seem safer than conflict in its usual sense. We get into them to test our skill, toughness, and presence of mind under pressure. And we do so voluntarily (although children are sometimes coerced into competitive activities for which they have little appetite). By befriending conflict, we need not participate in special activities to get these benefits. Any conflict can be an opportunity to hone our skill, presence of mind, and resiliency.

Conflict differs from competitive activities of other kinds because it follows no rules. It is up to each of the individual opponents to know his or her bottom line. Conflict without rules is unsafe. It is said that martial arts masters will not fight beginners because it is too dangerous for the masters. They are bound by rules and ethical principles that forbid them to willfully injure their opponents. Beginners, or those not schooled in the martial arts, are unlikely to have these constraints. Therefore, a master may put her life at risk by fighting with someone less skilled, but without these limitations. Her opponent, thinking the master to be all-powerful, may feel free to use all his unrestrained strength against her, even "fighting dirty" because he feels there is no way to win by fighting clean.

WHAT MAKES CONFLICT UNSAFE?

Almost everyone would agree that escalation is one of the most dangerous outcomes of conflict. Even the most minor dispute can quickly grow into open warfare. I have hinted, in the previous chapters, that underestimating our own strength can lead to escalation. We will explore how that escalation happens in much more detail in this chapter. We will also see how making conflict safe is much easier when we are in contact with our own source of inalienable power. As long as we locate our power by comparing our rank to that of our opponents, we are likely to identify too strongly with being victims and to inadvertently escalate conflict past the point of friendliness and even safety.

Escalation in its commonest form is symmetrical – by the time a conflict is well developed, it is difficult to say who started it and which side is responsible for it getting nasty. There are other ways that people get hurt in conflict that are not so symmetrical, as in the case of abuse.

No defense: When conflict turns abusive

Many of us avoid conflict because we fear that it will turn abusive. Abuse occurs when one opponent uses so much force, either physical or psychological, that the other cannot defend him- or herself.

Abuse is an emotionally loaded term. In a way, it has little to do with conflict because, in essence, one person is so overpowered that he or she cannot respond at all to the attack. But in another way, we can view abuse as one extreme of all conflict.

In the last chapter, we saw how the amount of strength we bring to a conflict depends on our goal. If we are intent on winning regardless of the effects on ourselves and our opponent, then we are prepared to push things to the point where our opponent can no longer defend him- or herself. The opponent who does not include safety and human relationship in his or her goals has at least the intent to abuse the other guy.

Whereas escalation may make conflict more overtly destructive in the moment, successfully overpowering an opponent leads to longer-term, more covertly destructive consequences.

When one opponent in a conflict "successfully" over-powers the other, it is only a temporary situation. Sooner or later, the "weaker" side will seek vengeance against the victor, possibly in the form of covert or terrorist-like retali-ation. It may take more than one generation for the reac-tion to emerge; revenge can be extraordinarily patient.

Overpowering an opponent also supports bullying, as we saw in Chapter 8. When we are overpowered, we are likely to take it out on someone we perceive as weaker than we. That is why it is so hard to learn from abuse. Against all of our desires, our experience of being unable to defend ourselves is likely to get passed down the line.

Furthermore, identifying too strongly with being a vic-tim frees us to use unbridled power on those we see as stronger than ourselves. If I don't see my own victimhood as a role, I am likely to see everyone as stronger than I. I will then remain unaware of my corresponding role as a perpetrator of abuse.

ESCALATION

As we've seen, one of the greatest hazards in conflict is escalation. It seems that even the tiniest disputes can turn into angry, hurtful, vindictive battles in which everyone gets hurt and the original problem gets magnified instead of resolved.

Let's take a look at some of the factors that contribute to escalation, so that we can do our part before engaging in conflict to keep things from getting out of hand.

Although any conflict can spiral out of control, there are some that take only a spark to turn into a wildfire. Conflicts that happen against a background of tension between individuals or groups escalate more easily than those whose opponents have less history together. Sometimes this tension is the result of earlier, unfinished conflicts. It can come from avoiding conflict over long periods of time. Or it can come from negotiated solutions to earlier conflicts in which both sides gave up too much (in their eyes) for the sake of temporary peace.

Befriending conflict – working on conflict in yourself before engaging with an opponent – can help clear up at least part of the atmosphere before things get out of hand. It can enable you to start with a cleaner slate, so that you enter the conflict with less history to cloud your mind and heart.

Tense atmospheres are bits of history that are kept alive in us as ghosts – the traces of old conflict that we carry with us as inner voices and fantasies, and in our dreams. That is why working on inner opposition and ghosts helps improve the atmosphere – it frees us to face our opponents as they are, not only as representatives of old, unresolved conflicts. The conflict may still escalate, but at least the soft rainfall of awareness may keep the fire from spreading as quickly.

ESCALATION AND POWER

Failure of each side to realize its own power is the fuel on which escalation feeds. In the previous chapter we saw how difficult it is to judge one's own power, particularly in the heat of conflict. Let's take a closer look at how misjudging one's own power inevitably leads to escalation.

My conflict with the hotel desk clerk is a perfect example. I felt victimized by the hotel. They were charging me an exorbitant fee for a room that turned out to be uninhabitable (if you recall, the toilet overflowed at 2 A.M.)! The ground was fertile for escalation – we had already been denied a room in another hotel at which we were sure we had a reservation. I felt powerless – as though the hotel business in general, and this hotel in particular, held all the cards.

When I complained to the desk clerk the next morning, she reacted from her role as a representative of the hotel. She did not attempt to see the situation from my viewpoint but stood on her power to charge me the full room fee. Why might she have done this? People generally identify with their roles when they feel insufficiently powerful to deal with others in ways they themselves might find ethical. She might have felt compassion for me and Kate and our horrendous lack of accommodation at "her" hotel, but felt she didn't have the authority to give me a discount. She even said that we had to speak with the manager – implying that the manager role did have sufficient power – but that the manager wasn't in. So she, while identifying with having insufficient power, used the authority of her role to overpower me. She had unconsciously escalated the conflict by supplementing what she perceived as her weakness with the authority of her role.

I, of course, felt overpowered – she had, in my view, failed to listen to my complaint. She did not even empathize with me. So I then felt free to ratchet up the power by another notch. I raised my voice – allowed myself to express my anger – and then violated her physical space by reaching across the desk and grabbing my credit card slip.

From the outside (Kate later told me), it looked really scary – two strong people using more and more power with one another until things nearly grew violent. And yet I (and presumably the clerk) each felt overpowered by the other!

This is the fundamental dynamic of escalation: Each side feels weaker than the other and therefore justified in applying yet more power until it defeats the other, apparently more powerful side.

In this case, both I and the desk clerk then de-escalated; I, by leaving (more accurately, storming out of) the hotel, and she by not calling the police. I – and presumably she – felt that to go any further would be too scary or counter-productive. And yet it was not the kind of de-escalation that made anyone very happy. It is likely that each of us passed on a bit of the conflict to others in our respective worlds that day.

GLOBAL ESCALATION

My conflict with the hotel clerk is remarkably similar to the nuclear arms race that nearly destroyed the world in the 1960s. Both the United States and the Soviet Union each believed they were in danger of being destroyed by the other. So each felt the only way of surviving was to build more nuclear weapons than the other side. In retrospect, this approach seems more like lethal idiocy, but at the time, each side merely thought it was defending itself against a stronger opponent!

ESCALATION AND ABUSE

Subjectively, I felt I had been abused by the hotel. I'd been put in a position against which it was impossible for me to defend myself. In my eyes, I had been treated unjustly. And yet no one took responsibility for mistreating me. I felt I was battling a ghost and therefore was completely justified in attacking a human representative of the hotel. I acted out of a sense of desperation – at not being able to defend myself against the hotel's seemingly arbitrary and unlimited power to make our time there—for which we were paying dearly—utterly miserable. In a way the hotel did deserve my wrath –it had no one on staff to deal with the inevitable discontent that must be its lot on a regular basis, if the conditions we endured were indicative of the hotel's overall service record. Who could blame me for insisting that the clerk – the only one I could interact with – compensate me for the sins of her employer?

On her side, the hotel clerk probably felt abused by me. She was in the position of a "flack-catcher," someone who stands between the hotel and the public, absorbing all the attacks that are really intended for the management! She, like many who interact with the public under unfavorable conditions, may have had to harden herself to put up with a constant stream of complaints (but little appreciation when things went well) from a disaffected public.

Escalation, in this case, stemmed from my feeling of having been abused. I was merely defending myself, in my own eyes, against a hotel management so powerful that I had to give up my personal ethics in order to defend myself. I completely failed to see myself as an aggressor until the whole show was over, whereupon I felt awful about what I had done.

It is characteristic of nearly all escalating conflicts that each side sees itself as a victim of the other. It sees its escalation, even when it turns violent, as a meager effort at self-defense. And this is as true of deadly international conflict as it is of my disputes with family, friends, and neighbors!

ESCALATION AND VALUES

When I see escalation as merely a matter of self-defense against a stronger opponent, I am likely to forget my bottom line – the values and ethical principles that ordinarily guide my actions. I consider myself a fair person. I am likely to tell a waiter when he or she has undercharged me, because I know he or she will get into trouble if I don't.

I try not to lose my temper with those over whom I have power, but if I do, I tend to feel remorseful and try to make things right between us. But when I feel overpowered, I tend to forget this sensitivity to my own and my opponent's feelings. More primal emotions emerge, and I feel like I am fighting for my life. I have learned that an essential step to making conflict safer is finding a reliable way of remembering my values, even in the midst of conflict.

These values might seem noble, but they might also be very practical. I once felt I had been unjustly treated by my academic advisor during my post-graduate studies. In my eyes, he had all the power, while I had to suffer silently through his moods and rages. I forgot that I was dependent on him for my salary, as well as my academic future. In my passion for justice, I unleashed my wrath on him—which proved a mistake, because I promptly lost my job! From my viewpoint, I had lost twice: I felt no closer to justice, plus my future suddenly looked bleak. I "solved" the problem by writing him a confessional letter in which I agreed with all his accusations and told him that I would like to continue my studies, even if he couldn't pay me. Nevertheless, the unfinished conflict left a lasting mark. I still feel resentful of him, even though our paths have long since diverged.

Aside from underestimating my own power, losing touch with my bottom line – my care for the well-being of my opponent as well as myself – in the heat of conflict is the strongest factor in making conflict unsafe. When I abandon these values, the conflict becomes unsafe for both me and my opponent, since I could, if pressed, muster all my available power to win, no matter who gets hurt.

POWER AND ETHICS

Conflict is made dangerous not so much by power but by its lack! When I am in touch with my own strength – with my source of inalienable power – I become a safer opponent. I have a reliable connection with something that no one can take from me, no matter how much of my property, my wealth, or my reputation they may take. I will fight for what is mine, but I will fight fairly. Having a stable reference point in myself, I will be able to better judge when I am overstepping my own values, my own ethical bottom line.

I consider it an ethical responsibility, rather than a luxury, to stand in my own power. If I stand only in my weakness, I am likely to support just those things that make me feel unsafe. For those of us who have been treated badly by life, it is understandable to want compensation. But identifying too strongly with our victimhood is unhealthy, not only for ourselves but for the world at large. For that reason, making sweet lemonade of even the sourest of lemons is not only a responsibility but a gift and a blessing to society, to our opponents, and to ourselves alike.

The following exercise will help you identify the aspects of a conflict that you find safe and ways to make that conflict safer for you and your opponent. After I present the exercise, Janice will take us through the steps to find out how to make the upcoming confrontation with her boss safer for her, her boss, and for the young man over whom they are about to clash.

EXERCISE: MAKING A FEARED CONFLICT SAFER

1. **Go through your conflict journal until you find an impending conflict that you feel could be unsafe** and would like to make safer.
2. **What do you fear most** in the conflict?
   - If you fear your opponent's strength, try to observe how this strength expresses itself in his or her body. Pay particular attention to how your opponent's posture, stance, and movement. Play with "shape shifting" into your opponent by trying out these physical

expressions, and notice if you can identify some of the strengths you perceive in your opponent as your own.

- If the situation reminds you of previous experiences (ghosts of conflict past), try facing and working on those experiences in the inner theatre of conflict – as you did in the exercise at the end of the chapter on busting ghosts (Chapter 7).
- If you fear escalation, experiment with finding the totality of your own power, including aspects of your psychological and spiritual rank that you otherwise might not recognize in yourself.
- If you fear you will become abusive of your opponent, take some time to understand your bottom line, what you are really hoping will come out of the conflict, deeper even than any possible material gain or loss.

3. **Now go deeper into your own experience** by finding the source of your inalienable power.

4. **Experiment with finding power in your body** that cannot be touched by comparison with others.

5. **Consider your relationship to spirit** – whether through specific spiritual or religious practice, through a deep knowledge that has no particular outer format, or possibly through your relationship to nature.

6. **Remember some of the difficult and dangerous experiences through which you have lived.** What enabled you to survive them? Take some time to find that resource as part of your current experience of yourself.

7. **What is your most fundamental attitude toward life?** Toward other human beings? What would remain if

you were to lose all your worldly possessions and all of the people who are important to you?

8. Make a movement or micromovement with your body or some part of it that will remind you of your inalienable power. Make a sketch that will help you remember it. In addition, you could make a sound, sing a song, or think of a place that will help you maintain contact with this power, even if the going gets rough.

9. Now, keeping in touch with the experiences that "anchor" your awareness of your inalienable power, go back to your anticipation of the conflict that you fear. How does maintaining contact with your inalienable power influence your attitude toward the conflict?

JANICE: DEFUSING A DANGEROUS CONFLICT

"Although I found an inner source of power that I believe will sustain me through my impending confrontation with my boss, I am still a little concerned about one or both of us hurting the other. This could make the already difficult emotional climate even worse. So let's try the exercise..."

A conflict I'd like to make safer: As I described in the last chapter, I'm upset that my boss is not supporting me to bend the rules for one of our kids, who I believe is in danger of falling through the cracks of the system. As much as I'd like to win this one, I don't want anyone to get hurt.

What I fear most in the upcoming conflict: I'm afraid of several things. If my boss wins, the kid may join the ranks of thousands of his brothers and eventually wind up on the street or in jail. If I win, I'm afraid of my boss's eventual retaliation. I could lose my job or be forced out by his making life impossible for me. And to be perfectly honest, I'm afraid of my own power – I feel so passionate about this that I could wind up hurting my boss so deeply that it might turn him completely away from his profession – which, given his gifts, I think would be a loss for all of us.

I fear my boss's strength—his structural power to push through his view of the matter. I see that strength in his relaxed stance and stillness when he is in his office. When I "try on" this relaxed style of movement, it reminds me of the relaxed but powerful body experience that I contacted in the exercise in the previous chapter. I then recognize that I share a measure of self-assurance with him that I also derive from my sense of confidence when I am succeeding in my work

Does it remind me of previous experiences? Yes, it reminds me of my power struggles with my mother. At the time, I had to break free of her to assert my own power, which I think hurt her more than she admitted. Remembering this reminds me of the potential to hurt my boss, especially if I were to confuse his professional responsibility with what I felt was my mother's arbitrary exercise of power over me.

Do I fear escalation? I'm afraid that if I lose the conflict, I'd be tempted to go over my boss's head, to his boss. And that would be, effectively, a declaration of war that could damage our whole agency. If I'm even thinking about going over his head, I must feel too weak to face him. I have to remember the psychological power I get from my passion for social justice, and how this can inflame those who feel put down by my ardor. I can imagine that when I am unconscious of my righteousness, it provokes unnecessary resistance from my boss, who I know also shares my passion for justice.

Could I become abusive to my boss? If I lose touch with my care for him, and focus only on what I believe is right for our client, I could imagine putting my boss up against the wall in a way against which it would be difficult for him to defend himself. This reminds me that social justice applies to everyone, not just to the ones I see as underdogs. Going still deeper, I realize that identifying my endangered client only as an underdog devalues him and could diminish his sense of empowerment. In this situation, everyone's boat has to float, or else.

Finding and anchoring my relationship to my inalienable power: While doing this, I will try to remember the experiences I had in the previous exercises, in which I also explored aspects of my inalienable power.

Power in my body: I've identified at least two sources of power in my body, which I now reconnect with by actually feeling them once more. One was the relaxed readiness – the slightly bent bow – with which I got in contact in the exercise in the last chapter. And I've also identified a kind of still relaxation that I see in my boss, that I don't always identify with in myself. It reminds me of the power of my position in the agency, and my ability to get things done.

Power through my relationship to the spirit: I do not practice any organized religion, but I have an almost spiritual reverence for non-violent leaders who have produced large-scale social change while remaining absolutely true to their personal values, no matter how powerful the opponents they faced.

Power through my difficult experiences: I feel that surviving my depressed home life as a child and young woman, as well as the bullying I endured at school, toughened me against heavy emotional atmospheres and personal attacks. I became quite familiar with the limits of my endurance, as well as how to take care of myself when those limits are surpassed. I am aware that this makes me seem a formidable opponent to those who oppose me. My ex-husband, my daughter, and my co-worker Charly can all testify to that!

My most fundamental attitude toward life and my fellow humans: I feel that a life that is cruel to others is not worth living. Although it might be necessary to temporarily hurt some to protect others, I feel that life is only worth living if I make social justice a principle for all beings, not just for the downtrodden. If I were to lose all my possessions and all the people I value or love, I believe I could still be happy if I were working for the good of all.

Movement, sketch and song to remind me of my inalienable power: I notice a subtle straightening of my spine, which I believe is almost invisible to an observer. I could do this anytime, any place to remind me of my deepest strength. The picture of the bow, slightly bent, still conveys this power to me. A "song" that helps me anchor this experience is the short sound "hmmhh," made with my mouth closed, that goes along with the subtle straightening of my spine with which I started this section.

Bringing it back to my conflict: Now, when I contemplate the upcoming conflict, I feel myself relaxing into my posture of power, like the bent bow. I feel how this frees me to focus more on my values and on my relationship to my boss, rather than on simply winning. I believe now that remaining in touch with my strength will also enable me to value him and his underlying desire for social justice. I believe that I can be more of a colleague to him and less of an opponent. Perhaps if I don't go in expecting a fight, we can actually cooperate toward solving this problem, for which we're both seeking a fair and useful solution.

ITCHING FOR A FIGHT —
ADDICTION TO CONFLICT

Clint Eastwood played many "tough guy" roles in the movies. His signature line in response to a threatened attack from a bad guy was, "Make my day!"

What an odd response to an attack! We usually want to flee rather than fight when someone threatens us with violence. Eastwood's attitude was fascinating because it expressed a forbidden feeling that most of us have had from time to time. We are in a mood – angry, perhaps bored, depressed, or feeling physically unwell—and would love nothing better than to get into a fight with someone.

This impulse is not always conscious or intentional. We may give grouchy, sarcastic answers to innocent questions. We may pick on our parents, our kids, our partner, or our friends until they react with sharp words or gestures. And then the fun starts. Before we know it, we're in the midst of a heated argument, our blood is boiling, we are shouting – and we feel oddly relieved, even though we have opened up a Pandora's box of trouble that we'll have to clean up later. The other person has "made our day" by giving us a way to blow off steam.

Moods have many different origins. They are often left over from previous conflicts that ended unsatisfactorily. We either gave up too much or perhaps shied away from the conflict, even though it was important to our self-interest or a valuable relationship. Another important source of moods is a subtle, longstanding depression that may be linked to the feeling that life has lost its meaning. No matter where a mood comes from, conflict promises to break up its monotony by giving us something solid—or fiery— with which to grapple.

Depression, for instance, can be so deadening that activity – any activity – can offer enormous, if temporary, relief. But because, in the midst of a depression, we seldom have the energy to initiate conflict, it is easier to get someone else to start it, giving us an easy way to get involved without being the bad guy– after all, the other person started it!

Physical symptoms that spread a diffuse sense of unwellness over us, such as springtime allergies, the first symptoms of the flu, or chronic arthritic pain, may make us grouchy, especially if there's not much we can do to relieve them. We feel under attack by invisible forces that we are powerless to influence. We take our medicine and wait it out. Wishing we could grab the real culprit, we lash out at anyone who comes within striking distance.

Perhaps the most difficult mood to deal with comes from leading a tough, perhaps disappointing, and (in our view) meaningless life. We feel that life owes us something. We cannot escape a feeling of being underprivileged, victimized by the world at large. Between possible bouts of depression, we are on the lookout for compensation, for justice. We want what we feel is rightfully ours. And because that has been taken away by the world at large — by fate or chance, or perhaps even, in our view, God — we have no one we can face directly to get back what the world owes us. We are ready to fight with anyone whom we experience as taking even the smallest thing from us. It is temporarily relieving to have a flesh-and-blood opponent to stand in for the world that has betrayed us, upon whom we can exert some of that pent-up strength with which we ordinarily cannot identify.

Having seen how moods contribute generally to feistiness, let's take a closer look at three different processes that are frequently connected with moods and that were hinted at in previous chapters: anger, revenge, and addiction to conflict. We will look at each individually, and then, at the end of the chapter, take a look back to see if we can come up with a general way of befriending even these otherwise unlovable aspects of conflict.

ANGER — AT WHOM?

I spoke earlier of my paternal grandfather — how he was perpetually angry because his life goals had been frustrated. As an educated but penniless immigrant, he was forced to work at menial jobs to scrape together enough money to make a better life for his family. He had nobody but abstract social injustice to blame for his plight. The twin ghosts of poverty and anti-Semitism conspired against his higher ideals. So he lashed out at anyone within striking distance, blaming his family and the minor irritations of everyday life for his long-term difficulties. My interest in him is more than historical. His legacy to his family was his rage. Both his son – my father – and I were heir to his explosive temper.

I experience anger as a wave that suddenly washes over me. Like the sea, it mutters quietly in the background, seldom completely still. And then, something happens that disturbs the quiet, and the wave swells. I feel annoyance growing in me like hot acid in my stomach. Unless I intervene at that point – at the very least become aware of and acknowledge that I am getting angry- the wave is likely to break. Typically, my tongue sharpens, injecting sarcasm into my speech. It is a subtle and unwarranted form of attack that leaves others confused and slightly hurt.

How can I befriend that anger? There are three steps:

1. **Remember Vitamin Awareness.** Notice that I am getting upset before the wave breaks. I have learned to read the signs of the swelling wave – I get impatient, my muscles twitch, I can barely sit still. Becoming aware of those initial signs is more than half the battle. Now what to do with that knowledge?

2. **Look for and address the ghosts.** This is one of the three basic steps toward befriending conflict that we met in the beginning of this book. I ask myself, what was it that upset me about the present moment? Ahhh...I felt the other person was oppressing me by making rules about what I should and shouldn't do. Hmmm...reminds me of my parents ... actually, reminds me of myself, always making rules about what's acceptable and what isn't.

3. **Differentiate your ghosts and their world from the person you're with.** If the ghosts made you feel helpless – as did my father, when he was in a negative mood – find your immediate sense of competence and ability. If the ghosts made you feel afraid, estimate your danger in this moment, with this person.

These steps all require awareness. They acknowledge your basic wisdom, that given all the information, you can choose how and where to exert your power. If, in the end, you feel that it is necessary to get angry at the person, you will at least deliver a dose of anger that is appropriate to the situation at hand. You will not have saved up a mega dose – fit for generations of family oppressors – for this one person.

Becoming familiar with – befriending – your own anger has an added benefit. You will have more compassion for the anger of others, even when it is aimed at you. Like my father who bought me a candy bar, putting an end to my rage toward my sister, you will stand a better chance of getting to the root of anger, rather than simply being its target.

REVENGE

On a scale of popularity, revenge sits way below anger. Revenge is considered uncool, no matter how delicious it may seem at the moment. Revenge serves many functions, the most obvious being an attempt to level the playing field. It is a crude way of snatching what we think of as justice when we feel we have been treated badly and have not been able to stand up for our own position. Revenge is a strategy for taking back something of equal or possibly greater value, in exchange for what we lost at an earlier time. Usually, we raise the stakes in revenge – we give back more pain than we suffered, we take back something more valuable than what was taken from us. Revenge is like a court settlement of a grievance in which you take from your opponent what he or she stole, plus "damages" – added money to compensate for the pain and suffering produced by his or her misdeed.

Because revenge is nearly impossible to defend against, coming, as it does, at time when we least expect it, it is usually abusive. Some of the most painful acts of terrorism are motivated by vengeance for real or imagined wrongs.

Revenge is difficult to befriend because it is easier to see its futility and destructiveness than it is to sympathize with its motivation. Revenge is motivated more by passion than by reason. The main purpose of revenge is to satisfy our need for vengeance!

Anger can be functional when it motivates us to action. Even when a good deal of anger is misplaced, it at least communicates to its target the depth of my discontent with him or her. It is immediate and can therefore be dealt with in the moment. Revenge, however, is always left over from an earlier event. One would think there should be an appropriate time in which to accustom ourselves to unjust loss, like a culturally accepted period of grieving for the dead. Unfortunately, injustice seldom dies; it just falls into a restless sleep from which it is easily awakened.

BEFRIENDING REVENGE

To be compassionate toward revenge requires, for many of us, somewhat of a shift in belief system. We need to look below the surface of unpleasant emotions to the source of emotion itself.

We saw, in the case of my paternal grandfather, that free-floating anger can result from a life of disappointment and suffering. We can understand that experience, because all of us have been angry or at least frustrated at one time or another. We also know firsthand that if we try to analyze anger too quickly, we can further inflame the emotion whose surface we are trying to penetrate. We can befriend emotions as a whole by realizing that they seldom, if ever, follow rational principles. To befriend emotion is to acknowledge something of our deeper nature, to be tolerant and patient with our more irrational impulses, knowing that they are a fundamental, if sometimes unwanted, part of us. No matter how disturbing or unwelcome they may seem, they almost always carry a seed of truth.

Revenge, like any emotion, can be a doorway to awareness. When we notice the impulse for vengeance, we can start by saying, "Hi, there...aren't you familiar!" And then, having accepted that we thirst for vengeance, we can backtrack to find out where it started. And that, in turn, could (but needn't) turn into an opportunity for re-opening the relationship with the person against whom we seek revenge. We then have the option of substituting relationship for vengeance.

My boundary conflict with my neighbor Jerry, which I explored in earlier chapters, began to degenerate into a vendetta — a drawn-out cycle of attack and revenge. But, since I didn't want to live with the tension of planning my revenge and avoiding his, I opted for improving our relationship. That inspired me to meet him face-to-face, discuss our common interests, and hammer out together a sustainable resolution in which both his and my interests were protected.

Revenge, for all its emotional impact, is seldom satisfying. First, it seeks to redress an injustice that is often so far in the past that what has been taken from you can seldom be reclaimed, even with the best efforts on the part of all parties. And secondly, because it is a response to something that happened in the past, it always appears to be unjust. And because it appears unjust, it tends to trigger counterrevenge by its target. So revenge turns into an escalating spiral of attack and counter-attack, often spread out over months, years, or even lifetimes.

Because revenge is seldom satisfying, it becomes addictive, much in the way that any almost satisfying experience can be addictive.

A SIDELIGHT ON ADDICTION

It is fashionable to see addiction as a physiological process. The substance or behavior we crave releases a hormone that makes us keep going back for more. This model downplays the importance of the subjective experience that the addiction gives us.

Addictions all share a common consequence. The substance or behavior we crave never quite satisfies us. It promises satisfaction, and may provide an initial kick or buzz, but then fails to deliver. The effect of the substance itself may become unsatisfying, which happens when we become habituated to it. Then taking the substance staves off the negative effects of not taking it but no longer delivers the same kick that got us hooked in the first place. Or it could be that along with the effects we crave, there are so many negative consequences that they overwhelm the benefits we get from the substance.

These two experiences together make a substance or behavior addictive: The substance or behavior promises satisfaction but fails to deliver on it. The longer it keeps the promise alive despite its failure to deliver, the more addictive it is.

Revenge promises satisfaction. If I can only show my tormentor how it felt to be his (or her) victim, I will finally feel satisfied. And at first I may indeed be satisfied. Revenge, as the saying goes, is sweet. But it is not sustainable. For my former tormentor, now my victim, will of course need to turn the tables once more by escalating the conflict. So what started off as satisfying has now turned into a long-term burden. The side effects soon overwhelm the initial burst of satisfaction. But if I could just deliver one more round, the definitive response, then....ecstasy! But of course, all I do is ratchet up the stakes another notch. If I am not careful, I can unleash a full-scale vendetta. And then my life will no longer be my own. It will be devoted, like a heroin addict to a fix, to maintaining the vendetta.

Keeping with our goal of adding Vitamin Awareness to conflict, I need to take into account not only the short-term satisfaction but also the long-term consequences of actually carrying out revenge.

ADDICTION TO CONFLICT

The insight we get from looking at the addictive quality of revenge can also serve our understanding of how conflict itself can be – and often is – addictive. Whenever conflict avoids its true target, it risks becoming addictive.

We saw how this works when we start a conflict with the wrong guy – when we inadvertently act like a bully. We have a disagreement with someone we see as too powerful to argue with, and instead take it out on someone who seems easier to defeat. This attempted solution cannot be satisfying in the long run because it doesn't address the initial conflict—which hovers in the background, stimulating more and more acts of bullying. I may get initial satisfaction by taking out my anger on someone I see as weaker than myself. I get the chance to win for a change, to get a sense of my own power. But it doesn't last. I still know in my heart that there is something more important, if more daunting, waiting for me.

Conflict is also addictive when we transfer our fight with ghosts onto real people. This can happen when we confuse our inner with our outer opponent. We fight with the guy on the outside, but are still stuck with inner opposition. So we have to keep fighting the same fight over and over again, without really touching the inner opponent, who is by far more destructive than the outer.

Just as taking more heroin cannot resolve a heroin addiction, we cannot break the vicious cycle of addiction to conflict just by getting involved in more conflict! This is one case where avoiding conflict is useful, even necessary. But avoiding conflict is only the first step, not the ultimate goal. We need to go further, or else the craving for conflict will remain and trip us up when we're least expecting it. As in any addiction, we must go to the root cause of the craving if we are to break the cycle of yearning and the incomplete satisfaction offered by the substance.

If, after getting to the root of our yearning, conflict still seems to be the way to achieve the satisfaction we seek, we may then practice a modified form of safe, non-addictive conflict by keeping our eyes and hearts on the ultimate goal, rather than the momentary satisfaction offered by immediate, no-holds-barred fighting.

What do we yearn for that conflict promises to satisfy? Typically:

- Justice – the feeling that we or someone important to us is being treated fairly by peers and superiors.
- Security – the sense of being safe in our home, community, or nation, without having to constantly defend it against those who seem stronger than us and who believe that what we have is rightly theirs.
- Contentment – the sense of having enough resources to sustain a good life, without having to take what belongs to others.

- Recognition – that we, as individuals, as well as whatever groups we draw our identity from, are recognized as worthy, equal members of society.

These basic needs lie at the root of all conflict, from family and neighborly disputes all the way to armed insurrection and war. As long as we keep our eye on what we really crave, we can avoid the trap of addictive – that is, unending, escalating, vindictive – conflict by aiming straight for what will satisfy us. We can never guarantee complete satisfaction – that would make life dull. But we can avoid the greatest pitfall of conflict escalating into pain and suffering, with no hope for resolution – by remaining keenly aware of what we really crave, and when that craving is satisfied, if only in small measure, and no matter how temporarily.

In addition to helping you gain an overview of your world of conflict experiences, the following exercise will give you an opportunity to process any tendencies you might have toward addiction to conflict. After that, we'll watch Janice going through the steps of the exercise.

EXERCISE:
RECOGNIZING AND WORKING ON AN
ADDICTION TO CONFLICT

1. **Review the range of actual and potential conflicts in your life.** See if you can find a pattern in them. Is there a particular kind of situation that is typical of several conflicts? Do you keep getting into conflicts with the same sorts of people? Take a few minutes to describe

that pattern. What do all those conflicts have in common?

2. **What are you yearning for in those conflicts?** What would satisfy you? It might be something quite irrational or that even seems childish. It might be a need for recognition, for love, for appreciation, or for security. Allow yourself to savor that need, even if it seems unattainable or embarrassing.

3. **How successful is your current approach to satisfying that yearning?** If it is not completely successful, where and how does your current approach fall short of satisfying it?

4. **Who could really satisfy that need?** It could be a real or imagined person, either from your actual life or perhaps a historical, spiritual, or mythological figure. Allow yourself to experience the satisfaction that that relationship promises you until you are satisfied you have gotten to the core of your yearning.

5. **Now go back to the first step of this exercise and select a typical conflict.** Does finding an inner source of satisfaction change your attitude toward this conflict? Does it suggest any new ways of approaching this pattern of conflict that could be more satisfying?

Now let's see how Janice applies these ideas to working on her addiction to confront conflict with her ex-husband and her boss.

JANICE: HARNESSING MY TEMPER

"I realize that I do have somewhat of an addiction to conflict! I have a reputation for having a fiery temper, and I believe that a mild conflict addiction is what gives rise to it..."

Looking for a pattern in my conflicts: Considering the range of conflicts I identified in the inventory at the end of the second chapter, I notice that they all revolve around the theme of responsibility. I have conflicts with my daughter, my ex-husband, and my co-workers. In each case, I stumble into a conflict while trying to protect someone – whether a client of our agency or my daughter – from life's dangers.

What I'm yearning for in these conflicts: I am yearning for a safer, more predictable life for everyone. I realize that only when I feel that everyone around me is safe can I feel secure. This is, of course, an impossible goal. While doing the exercises in the previous chapters, I realized that I can be dangerous to the very people I'm trying to protect. But that doesn't make me yearn any the less for the safety of everyone. It appears that my yearnings and their effects may clash at times...

How I'm currently trying to satisfy that yearning: I have two approaches to trying to protect those who I feel are endangered. The first, which I use mostly with my daughter, is to lay down ironclad rules of behavior. This one doesn't work well, because I suspect that she sees me as a threat to her freedom. So this method is self-defeating, even counterproductive, as it intensifies my efforts to keep her safe. Hmmm...looks like it supports an addiction to conflict, since I get stricter and stricter the more she resists me.

A second approach, which I use on those I perceive as holding more power, like my ex and my boss, is to rebel against them, barely listening to their requests and arguments before pushing through my version of how things ought to be done. This, of course, strengthens their will to push through their version, and we wind up, predictably, in an escalating conflict. Here, too, my approach not only falls short of satisfying my yearning to protect the weak; it actually exposes them to greater risk by irritating those who hold power over them. And that greater risk spurs me to be even harsher with my boss or ex, which irritates them further…another vicious cycle that falls short of satisfying my yearning to protect my daughter and the agency's clients.

What could fully satisfy that yearning: I can't immediately think of a person who could satisfy that need for security, so maybe I'll have to rely on an inner experience. I remember the source of inalienable power I accessed while doing the exercise at the end of Chapter 9. While looking at the arc that I drew to express that power, I lean back and again feel that relaxed strength I felt it in the long muscles of my back and limbs. I find myself stretching lazily, like a lioness watching over her cubs who are playing nearby. As I watch and feel my way into her, I experience myself in a new way – as someone whose power is completely adequate to meet the challenges of her life. I see that lioness as someone who can defend her cubs – and herself – against any threat. And she does it not through aggression, but by just feeling secure and at home in her own body.

Applying this experience to a typical conflict: My upcoming confrontation with my boss is uppermost in my mind. I now realize that as much as I feared clashing with him, confrontation was the only way I knew to stand my ground with him. I'm beginning to wonder if my confrontational style of conflict has become a way of life because it's the only way I've been able to experience my power. My newly discovered lion-nature gives me an inspiration for a new way to conduct conflict. If my personal security were less at risk, I think I could focus better on the viewpoint I'm trying to get across.

This idea helps me refocus my attitude toward my larger goal in life: my yearning for social justice for all. I see that my larger battle is with social reality as a whole, but that I never felt strong enough to engage in it. It now dawns on me that my fellow social workers could become allies in that battle. To enlist them, I might need to see them more as a lioness would her cubs, rather than seeing them as my adversaries. I could be firm and directive, but at the same time protective of them, too. I could guide them by example, rather than by head-on conflict."

TAKING IT ON THE ROAD — BEFRIENDING REAL-LIFE CONFLICT

Up to now, we've been more concerned with rehearsing for, rather than engaging in, conflict. In this final chapter, we'll look at ways to use our new-found tools while we're in the midst of conflict. We'll find that they are every bit as useful for actually "doing" conflict as they are preparing for it.

What's the difference between rehearsal and performance? In rehearsal, we need deal only with our imagined opponent. Our feelings, trance states, and behavior may be just as real as during outer conflict, but we have time to go back and retrace our steps if the imagined sequence doesn't turn out as we want or expect. An actual opponent who is more intent on winning than on preserving our relationship would be smart to exploit our hesitation to help him- or herself to win.

In actual conflict, presence of mind is all-important. Whatever we do we need to do it quickly, or we will have nothing but raw power on which to fall back. In this sense, we are very much like the actor who prepares for a live performance by rehearsing for it. His goal is to make his performance automatic, so that he can focus on the finer points of the performance when he is finally on stage. He will be able to adapt to the mood and flow of the other actors as the play unfolds. He will not stumble over others' lost lines or missing cues, nor will he be thrown off if he forgets one of his own lines. Rehearsal will free him to reach for his artistic goals, rather than struggle just to keep up. Rehearsal keeps the actor nimble, able to deal with new and unexpected situations that arise during the performance.

ACTUAL CONFLICT

Engaging in a real outer conflict differs from rehearsal in several other ways. Your outer opponent is never as predictable as your inner version of him or her. You may imagine how this opponent will act in a general sort of way, but actual people are famous for stepping outside the box our mind puts them in. Because people are unpredictable, we cannot reduce conflict management to a simple formula.

But the possibility of unexpected outcomes is exactly the reason why conflict can be so invigorating. You may, at any moment, find yourself inexplicably touched by an opponent who, only moments before, you passionately disliked. New worlds of understanding may suddenly open to you, as you dive below the turbulent surface of a nasty conflict into a world of shared, even universal experience that leaves both you and your opponent in awe, changed forever. Or you may discover previously untapped resources in yourself that will transform your self-image from one of weakness to strength, from that of hapless victim to someone who is sufficiently powerful to help, rather than just fight, the opponent.

It would be tempting to use the tools we have been exploring in the previous chapters as a way of winning conflicts. They are not intended for that purpose. Rather, they will help you go into conflict as your whole self, leaving nothing behind. But bringing your whole self – your strengths and weaknesses, your mindfulness and your trance states, your generosity and your pettiness – into conflict is only half the battle. A further step is to retrieve that wholeness when, in the midst of conflict, you are attacked, whether from within or without.

In this chapter, we will focus on how to retrieve awareness that we typically lose when attacked. Losing awareness is both the fear that many of us bring into conflict and the often bitter experience that we have taken away from past conflicts. On the surface, losing awareness can set us up to lose the fight itself; in a deeper sense, we fear that it may strip us of our very humanity, leading us to do things that we may regret both during the fight and possibly for a long time thereafter.

WHO STARTED IT?

The concept of conflict, as we have seen, is a wide-ranging one, covering everything from mild disagreements to full-scale armed warfare. Volumes could be (and have been) written about every aspect of conflict, from waging war to making peace, from conquest to negotiation, from standing up for yourself to loving your enemy, and all points in between.

One factor that seems common to all conflicts, from the nursery to the global battlefield, is accusation. Conflicts start with one side accusing the other of some misdeed and then typically "settle down" to a cycle of accusation and counter-accusation.

Each side experiences the other's accusations as attacks upon its good intentions, its ethics, its humanity, and ultimately its very sanity. And although one side initially accuses the other of something concrete – physical injury, theft, violations of personal or national boundaries – the specific issues are soon overwhelmed by an argument over WHO STARTED IT.

In a typical round of accusation and counter-accusation, each side is likely to call its action a re-action to some earlier insult from the other side. We see this pattern in children's fights, where, in the middle of a hair-pulling match between two siblings, each tells the intervening parent, "She/he started it!" And we see it in armed conflict, where each side says it is simply reclaiming property, rights, or honor that has always been its but was taken from it by the aggressive opponent. These chains of accusation can span centuries, the sense of injustice so deeply ingrained on both sides that sorting out the tangled threads of cause and effect seems all but hopeless. Revenge soon takes its place beside accusation, ensuring that the conflict not only continues but escalates.

The similarity of wars with children's spats highlights the irrational, emotional side of even the deadliest of armed conflicts. Even when the stakes are incredibly high – the freedom, welfare, or survival of whole populations – conflict resolution won't last unless it deals with the emotions that stand behind the facts.

It may take a team of historical and political experts to clear the tangled mass of interests and rights that form the visible surface of conflict, like the twining branches and vines of a rain forest. But the very same tools we have been discussing throughout this book can be used by anyone, at anytime, to penetrate to the emotional roots that feed and support the surface issues.

ACCUSATION, TRUTH, AND RELATIONSHIP

When we are accused of wronging someone, our natural reaction is to deny the accusation. Consider the following all-too-familiar scenario.

The guy in back of me in line at the supermarket accuses me of slowing down the express checkout with my 12 items, two more than the "10 Items Only" printed clearly on a large overhead sign. How should I answer his accusation?

I feel falsely accused. I have four cans of tuna, and eight other items. I know that tuna is on special at four cans for three dollars. So I have been seeing my four cans of tuna as one unit of sale, and therefore as a single item. From my perspective, I am right and he is wrong. Since I believe I have objective truth on my side, my first impulse is to justify my actions. I am tempted to reply, "But there are four identical cans of tuna on special at four for three dollars, and eight other things. That's only nine items, really."

But from his perspective, he was right, since he didn't know about the special (and probably doesn't care), and he counts 12 items, not nine. There is no absolute standard of truth in this situation, only our conflicting points of view.[1]

Given that neither of us is objectively right, is the guy's accusation true or false? Should I or shouldn't I take it seriously? Since I'm not about to start a debate with him, I have to decide rapidly what to do, without any reliable standard of truth to fall back on. How should I answer his accusation? It appears that nothing I say can be completely true, so any answer seems inconsequential from the standpoint of truth or falsehood. But I know that my response will have consequences. It will affect the way my accuser and I relate to each other, as well as how each of us will feel after our encounter. This kind of situation can lead to a war of words, because my agreement or disagreement with my accuser has little effect on the truth, but significant consequences for both my and his self esteem.

If I say he's wrong, I am challenging the accuracy of his perception and attacking his credibility and his pride. This is bound to leave him feeling less than friendly toward me. It will leave a slightly tainted atmosphere between us, like a whiff of bad odor that may stay with both of us for a while.

If, on the other hand, I admit that he is right for the sake of making peace, I am being unjust to myself. It will look as though I was trying to pull a fast one on him and I come out looking bad. Admitting he is right might even escalate the disagreement, since it would give him grounds for looking down on me for attempting to deceive him.

There is another level of truth in this drama that refers not to who is right and wrong, but to the experience that led me to take the 12 items through the express checkout line. And it is a subtle truth that cannot be captured by "right" or "wrong."

If I am honest with myself, I have to admit that my accuser was a little bit right. I remember arguing with myself about whether I should take the express line since I, too, counted 12 individual items. I had to marginalize that perception in order to count them up and get nine. So even if I have succeeded in justifying my breaking the rule, I must admit there is a sense in which his accusation is a little true, even though in a court of law, the judge might find in my favor.

So my response to my accuser depends on my own bottom line, what I value most in relationship to him. If my highest value is being right, then I need to — and even, with relatively good conscience could — completely deny his accusation. I might even shore up my denial with facts that fit my view, as by asking the checker, the store manager, or another store employee to back me up — and hoping that they'll do it.

But if I am more interested in relating to my accuser in the interest of maintaining a good emotional atmosphere, I might tell my truth, which is that he is a little right. I might first tell him why I think I did the right thing, and then share with him my own uncertainty, and how I was in a hurry to get out of the store quickly, and how that led me to fudge just a little on the 10 items rule.[2]

In this rather trivial example, not much hinges on the outcome of my interaction with my accuser. At worst, each of us would have a somewhat unpleasant aftertaste from our encounter. But there are other accusations that are much more serious, where much more hinges on the outcome of the encounter between the accuser and the accused.

Conventional wisdom dictates that when the stakes are high, it is better to deny everything and let one's accuser prove his or her point. But in many situations, being candid about even a tiny grain of truth in an accusation can defuse an otherwise potentially dangerous conflict.

Because accusations are loaded by the clashing experiences of the accuser and the accused, deciding on their truth or falsity seldom solves the underlying conflict. It is therefore prudent to find the grain of truth in an accusation, no matter how small or inconsequential it may seem alongside of the "real" truth, whatever that may be.

ACCUSATIONS AND ATTACKS

When do accusations lead to fights? When we experience them as an attack. Then they are like the first punch thrown in a fight or the first shot in a battle. Accusations that lead to fights are the ones that hurt us, against which we need to defend ourselves. And our defense is usually more energetic than we intend it to be, especially when we underestimate our own strength.

Not all accusations hurt us – some are so absurd that we simply shrug them off.

A few years ago, Kate and I were walking down Seventh Avenue in New York after dinner, on a rainy spring night, enjoying the relief from the day's heat. A guy walked up beside us and said, "Who the hell are you? Why did you make it rain?" Our first reaction was to stiffen up and walk faster, hoping he would go away. But he didn't. He kept up, accusing us of being responsible for making it rain, of not knowing anything. I thought, "That guy is nuts!" We couldn't make it rain, even if we tried!

But he wouldn't leave; he kept walking alongside of us, hurling accusations our way. We realized there was nothing personal in his accusation, and since he wasn't going away, we decided to relate to him. He didn't appear to be violent, just energetic, so we tried relating to him in kind. We started walking as energetically as he was, and said, "What do you mean we made it rain? We didn't make it rain!" But he insisted, "You don't know anything! YOU MADE IT RAIN. MAKE IT STOP NOW!" We defended ourselves for a couple of rounds, and then I said to him, "You don't know anything!" And he looked us square in the eye and said "What do you mean I don't know anything? You don't know anything!" But now he was smiling. So we went back and forth like that for a while, all of us smiling and laughing and trading insults. And after a few more rounds he said, "You folks have a good night!" and went happily down the street. And then he encountered someone else and turned to him and said, "Who the hell do you think you are…making it rain like this…"

We didn't take his accusation as an attack because it was impersonal. It wasn't meant to hurt us — we could only guess that he was looking for someone who could relate to him with the energy that he felt inside. He was probably fighting with a ghost that was telling him he didn't know anything, that he was responsible for lots of things he couldn't possibly have caused. So it was relieving when we obliged by stepping good-naturedly into that role. We signaled by our laughter and willingness to engage him that we didn't really mean it – we were just standing in for an inner opponent and giving him a chance to finally confront it in person.

Other accusations cut clear to the bone. In those cases, finding a grain of truth in even the most unjust-seeming accusation can lessen the force of the most painful attack. Let's look at a situation that affected me much more deeply than my encounter with the guy who accused me of making it rain.

I was facilitating a seminar on personal growth, and someone stood up and said to me in a loud voice, "This seminar isn't safe. You are responsible for our safety, and it isn't safe here!" At the instant of this accusation, I felt like I'd gotten punched in the stomach. I was happy with how the seminar was going, most of the participants looked happy, and then this. It was an accusation, much like the guy accusing me of not knowing anything, but this time I felt personally attacked.

Accusations feel like attacks when they punch a hole in our reality. I was going along in a state of ease, satisfied with my teaching, when suddenly I was accused of making the seminar unsafe not only for one but all of the participants. My accuser implied that I was acting unethically – I was supposed to be helping the participants, not harming them.

Groups, especially those that focus on experiential learning, can feel unsafe to their participants for several reasons. Some participants fear that the facilitator will press them to reveal personal information that they'd rather keep private. Others are afraid that if they take a strong stand on an issue, they will be overly identified with that position by other members of the group. This can be especially risky if revelations made in the context of an experiential learning group are revealed in the person's workplace, or presented out of context to a friend who wasn't present at the time. Still others find that they take stronger positions, and stick to them more tenaciously in group situations, than they would in casual discussion with a few friends or co-workers. They may be seen by others in the group as overly contentious or uncooperative.

It is hard to learn in an atmosphere of fear. For this reason, I had devoted a lot of care to making sure that participants in my seminars felt safe emotionally. I knew that his accusation couldn't be literally true. So my first impulse was to deny his accusation completely. But to someone who already experiences the atmosphere as being unsafe, receiving a public counter-accusation from the leader of the seminar would only confirm his accusation. Just defending myself would clearly not work, no matter how justified I felt.

On the other hand, I felt so hurt by his public attack that I was almost ready to admit its truth if only to appease him, to get him off my back. But if I admitted he was right, I would also be implicitly admitting that my seminar was having the opposite effect from the one I intended. So

I would be admitting to being either incompetent, fraudulent, or an unsavory blend of both.

Whether I defended myself or admitted to his accusation, I would come out looking bad. I was trapped. No wonder I felt stunned!

FEELING STUNNED

Feeling "stunned" is a very special state of mind. I felt frozen, immobile, unresponsive, very much as though I had been physically knocked out by a blow to my head. I felt misunderstood, wronged, unjustly accused, but I stood there like an idiot, unable to defend myself or even answer my accuser.

Why was I stunned? After all, the guy who accused me of making it rain didn't stun me. I hardly knew the guy in my seminar, and surely had nothing personal against him. And yet, I felt hurt by him. I knew I could straighten things out if only I could get my damned mind back!

How did this situation differ from the rainmaker situation?

It was inconceivable to me that I could have caused the rain. That kind of accusation is not a "hot button" topic for me. But it was completely plausible that I could unintentionally bruise the participants in my seminar emotionally through inattention, unconsciousness, or worse still, through completely misjudging the effect of my presence on the group.

His accusation conspired with my own inner critical voices that murmur away in the background, questioning everything that I do.

I have made a certain peace with these voices. Through years of exploring my relationship to them, I have come to see them as allies, the echo of dissenting points of view that contribute to the richness and diversity of my worldview. I have come to know them as teachers, as sparring partners, even as friends. But it is an uneasy relationship even in the best of times. So when I am under attack, as I was then, they are easily recruited to the role of inner opponent.

Now I can understand why I felt stunned. At the moment of the attack, I focused inward, on my own experience, instead of outward, on my accuser. I fell into an inner discussion among various points of view. But the discussion left me "on hold." Everything was happening inside and not much was coming out.

I was dealing not only with an outer but also an inner accuser. It was a case of "two against one," just like I described at the beginning of this book. But now I was on stage, not rehearsing – this was opening night. The accusation came suddenly, unexpectedly. I needed a method to deal with it just as rapidly, so that I could turn my attention back to my accuser and to the group. Otherwise, my "absence" would lend a bit of support to his accusation – nobody would be minding the group while I was off on my inner journey.

How could I respond to both my inner and outer accusers quickly enough to satisfy him, but without making it emotionally unsafe for myself? After all, I was also part of the group, and if I felt unsafe, I would act defensively toward the group, making it feel less safe for them. I would unconsciously escalate the conflict. And if I covered over my own feeling of hurt, I would risk taking subtle vengeance on my accuser and, indirectly, on the group. I might become sarcastic, remote, or merely impatient. And this would sour the atmosphere even further, leading first to a subtle, and then an overt, escalation as the group and I slowly transformed into mutual opponents.

I now understand this dynamic as the kind of escalation that occurs when both opponents in a conflict underestimate their own power. I know, for instance, that when I feel hurt by a group, I forget how much power is invested in me by my position as leader and teacher, so I tend to react with much more force than is warranted by the situation. Similarly, members of a group tend to forget, when they feel attacked by the leader, how much force they have at their disposal. A few sarcastic remarks or an outrageous accusation can paralyze the most determined of group leaders. It is the formula for a perfect escalation that can make the most peaceful group seem dangerous for everyone, leaders and participants alike.

ACCUSATION WITHOUT ESCALATION

Why do accusations escalate? There is a simple but profound reason. There is always a bit of truth in even the most outrageous of accusations That guy on Seventh Avenue believed that I was responsible for the rain. But he expressed his belief as an emotionally charged accusation, not as a simple fact. It was my fault, not just my act. In his view, I had done something wrong — and that's why it rained. My first impulse was to think that he was crazy. In my world, I don't cause rain. And even if I did, how could I have known it would disturb him? After all, I'd never seen him till that moment.

It was natural, even logical, for me to deny his accusation. Yet by doing so, I told him, in effect, that his view of the world was incorrect. I called his grasp on reality into question. But that didn't change his perception one bit!

In that situation, my accuser's experience was true, regardless of the actual facts. No matter how extreme his experience may seem to us now, most of us at one time or another have experienced natural phenomena that disturb us as the "fault" of someone or something – be it spirits, a deity, a malevolent human being, or nature itself. No matter how hard our rational minds try to convince us otherwise, our perceptions, thoughts, beliefs, suspicions, and experience, in general, are as real to us as any scientific fact or mathematical proof. When he accused me of making it rain, I could admit to a grain of symbolic, if not literal truth to his accusation. In some sense, I was responsible for his irritation, as a member of an uncaring mainstream that marginalized his existence by judging his behavior as bizarre. I was ready to step into the role of something or someone that was irritating him, in order to give him a chance to satisfy what I guessed was his yearning for contact. It cost me nothing and gave both of us a moment of contact and satisfaction in an otherwise bleak and uncaring cityscape.

We could have avoided that dispute over the rain by walking away from our accuser. But in the moment, it seemed more interesting to engage him. Because we were not hurt by his accusation, we were free to join him in his world without animosity – and therefore, without escalation. We affirmed his experience by playing his game, even though, verbally, we disagreed with him.

This event underscores the role of conflict in making, rather than breaking, relationships. The key to relating to him constructively through conflict was our detachment from his actual accusation. We were good-natured rather than confrontational.

My accuser in the seminar no doubt felt genuinely unsafe, whether or not I intended to create a safe atmosphere. Indeed, he felt unsafe no matter what anyone else in the group felt.

I felt that the group was safe. No matter what anyone else felt or said, I believed that I had created a safe environment. Indeed, the fact that a participant was free to accuse me of creating an unsafe seminar confirmed to me that he felt safe enough to criticize me!

Clearly the two of us had very different experiences of exactly the same situation. Our contrasting viewpoints set the stage for at least a disagreement but potentially a full-scale conflict.

And yet, there was surely a grain of truth in his accusation. Since safety is largely a subjective experience, the mere fact that someone feels unsafe means that in at least a very small way, things are unsafe.

Many people feel unsafe in groups, for general reasons that I described earlier in this chapter. In addition, groups have a life of their own. Individuals who express points of view that conflict with the prevailing view of the group

may be shouted down without much respect for their feelings. Even groups that view themselves as democratic can
"vote down" the will of a substantial minority without
apology or remorse. And it is conventional, even justified,
to hold the leader or convener of the group responsible for
the group's acts. But in the end, safety is in the eye of the
beholder. An emotionally charged atmosphere may feel
life-threatening to one person but invigorating to another.

In the end, there is no absolute standard of safety.
Safety is a matter of mutual experience; what constitutes
safety for two or more people needs to be discussed and
even argued about. I have my view of what is safe, and you
have yours. But paradoxically, the more I try to push my
viewpoint that the group is safe, the less safe I make it for
someone who holds the opposite view! And if I push my
point even harder, then I may begin to feel unsafe, since
my leadership will be threatened by his ever stronger reaction. The only way that I can enforce my opinion of the
group's safety is by becoming tyrannical, which makes the
group unsafe for all those who are threatened by tyranny!

Of course, simply admitting that the group is unsafe —
that I have made it unsafe — does not solve the problem
either. Unless I show that I really appreciate and validate
my accuser's perception, my admission will sound hollow,
patronizing. I can make my admission genuine by saying
exactly how I contribute to the group's lack of safety.

There is no guarantee that my admitting to the grain of
truth in an accusation will satisfy my accuser. There are
many reasons for making an accusation, only some of
which have to do directly with the accusation's content.

The guy who accused us of making it rain was evidently looking for a playmate – someone to match his considerable energy. But until I can find the grain of truth in an accusation, particularly one that impacts me emotionally, I will not be fully present or able to help untangle the web of "he said, she said." Finding the grain of truth in an accusation helps me to clear my own mind, separating the wheat of responsibility from the chaff of rank, revenge, ghosts, and bullying. Until I find that grain of truth, I will be just as unsafe to myself as I perceive my accuser to be.

In light of that realization, let's take a look at a method for finding the grain of truth in even an absurd accusation. Then we'll follow up by considering some of the functions that accusations play in our relationships. Once we have the means to regain clarity, we come that much closer to harvesting the real riches from the fertile ground of conflict.

FIRST AID FOR ACCUSATIONS

There is, fortunately, a simple first aid measure for recovering your awareness when you stand accused of doing something wrong. It has several steps, each aimed at satisfying a particular part of your experience. I'll give the steps first, then we'll discuss why each is so important and how it helps you **recover from even the nastiest of accusations.**

1. **Defend yourself.** When you are accused, even if you suddenly realize that the accusation is valid, try standing up for yourself, if only for a brief moment. If you don't stand up for yourself even a little, the rest of the steps may be very difficult to complete, because your heart

won't be in it.

The most effective way of standing up for yourself is to reflect on how the accusation is false or at least incomplete. Even if the accusation has some truth to it, you didn't intend to be as nasty or harmful as you are being accused of. Standing up for yourself is like cleaning an injury before you bandage it. It helps prevent infection further down the line.

2. **Ask yourself, "Is it more important that I prove my innocence or that I keep a relationship with my accuser?"** This is a way of rapidly finding your most basic values in the conflict.

   Remember our discussion of the "bottom line" in the chapter on practicing safe conflict? We found that if you are intent on winning a conflict at any cost — including harm to your opponent — then you are in danger of escalating the conflict until everyone gets hurt. You can probably defeat your accuser, but the victory might be quite costly. Valuing relationship over victory is often the most sustainable policy. It saves you from making long-term enemies who can come back to haunt you when you least need it.

3. **If, in spite of these considerations, you opt for victory at all costs, then your job is done at this point.** But if you find that while winning, you regret the cost to your own peace of mind, it's never too late to come back to the next step....

4. **Ask yourself, "What part of the accusation is true, even if it is only a tiny bit, or in a very limited or specific way?"**

   If the accusation is zero percent true, it probably won't even bother you. Remember the guy who accused me of making it rain? It didn't bother me because it was so thoroughly absurd. It just wasn't true! But as soon as an accusation affects me emotionally, that tells me it's a little bit true. Otherwise it wouldn't affect me!

The smallest way that an accusation can be true is if I've accused myself of the same thing at some point. Then it is true for me if for no one else. Another way is if I've been accused of the same thing more than once. When I first began to lead groups, I was accused of neglecting safety on more than one occasion. Often I did this by defending one participant against an attack by another, not realizing that my unconsciousness of my own power had bruised the initial attacker. Where there's smoke, there's fire. So there must have been enough truth in that accusation for more than one person to have grabbed on to it.

I could surely blame my accuser for his reaction to me – he had a problem with authority, he felt too weak to deal with me straight, etc., etc., etc. But since I had already decided that it was more important to relate to him than to defeat him, I was willing to explore the way in which he could be right.

5. **Explain to your accuser exactly how he is right.**
   Remember, you've already told him how he isn't right. You've decided that relating to him is more important than winning, and you've found the grain of truth in his accusation.

   Bear in mind that you are telling your accuser what is right about his accusation in the interest of maintaining a relationship with him. For the message to get through to him, you must do this with your heart open to your accuser, and with your mind open to your accuser's reaction.

How My Accuser Was Wrong, and How He Was Right

Now let's see how I followed these steps when I was accused of making the seminar unsafe.

When I realized I was stunned by the accusation that the seminar was unsafe, I decided to go through my checklist.

First, where was his accusation false? Did I make things unsafe? No. My partner Kate and I had often discussed the issue of safety. We came to the conclusion that making rules about what people could and couldn't do in a seminar gave the appearance of safety but was ultimately unenforceable. And people were more likely to get hurt as a consequence of having rules imposed upon them. In the past, I had tried to impose a rule that participants should not criticize other participants who had just gone through emotional experiences in the group. But silencing participants in an effort to keep from hurting others hurt them. The attempt to "create" safety for one participant made it less safe for others. We therefore had only one bottom line rule. Participants were not permitted to physically attack one another. And we enforced this prohibition through our awareness and our actions, rather than by setting down a rule. We were responsible for participants' physical safety.

Next, what were my values, my bottom line? Was it more important to defend myself or to relate to the participant? I felt that I wanted to relate to the participant who had criticized me. I wanted to learn from his experience. If there was a way to make the atmosphere safer, I wanted to do it. At the same time, I was hurt by him. I wanted desperately to defend myself. Finally, I decided that the relationship was more important. I furthermore believed that forcing my opinion on him would actually validate his accusation – it would prove that it was unsafe for him to voice his opinions without getting overrun by my power!

Part of a good relationship, in my opinion, means honoring the other person's perception, even if I vigorously disagree with it. I know from bitter experience that nothing makes me feel worse than having my perception flat-out denied. No matter how absurd my perception, I feel crazy when another completely denies its validity. So I thought that defending myself too vigorously would indeed make the seminar unsafe for my accuser, no matter how safe I thought it was initially.

These considerations made it possible for me to take on the accusation to find the part of it that was justified. So next, I considered how the accusation might be true.

How did I make the situation unsafe? I realized that I had underestimated how traumatic public conflict was for many of the participants. I had developed a taste for spicy interaction over the years. Although I still found public accusations painful, I valued the opportunity to "walk my talk," to practice the conflict management skills that I'd been cultivating. I came to believe that awareness was more important than prescribed rules. But in my enthusiasm to learn from conflict, I failed to see my attitude toward conflict as a privilege that others might not share with me. I was willing to take risks in relationships that others saw as risky to the point of negligence. So I had to admit to my accuser that I had indeed failed to take his feelings into account, assuming that he was so eager to learn from conflict that he would be willing to risk some emotional bruising.

A Beginning, not the end

My explanation relieved me and him to the degree that we could proceed with the seminar. Indeed, it seemed to have made the space sufficiently safe that others began to stir up trouble of different sorts. And that, in turn, created a lively forum for on-the-spot learning. What started out as a rather routine teaching seminar turned into a kind of martial arts studio, where many participants got to try out their conflict management skills by vying with me and each other.

I was later told by several participants that they found the experience enlightening, and that furthermore, it had given them courage to work with large groups on challenging material. They saw a new pattern – instead of simply getting defensive, both the leader and the group could learn and grow from the experience. Facing safety head-on as a group issue created a more convincingly safe atmosphere than any set of rules and contracts could have done.

Oftentimes, however, accusations form the tip of a much larger iceberg. Finding and admitting to the grain of truth in the accusation doesn't solve the problem, but instead reveals deeper, more interesting layers of our relationship to our accuser.

Placing oneself in a position of strength and authority wakes a whole chorus of ghosts in those we deal with. As a politician, a leader, or even a therapist, we become objects of anyone who needs to test his or her power against a worthy opponent. When Harry Truman said, "If you can't stand the heat, stay out of the kitchen," he was referring to the need of those who put themselves in public positions to develop a tolerance, or even a taste for, the conflict that inevitably goes with the job.

I once got a call from a former therapeutic client who had broken off therapy several years earlier. She felt at the time that I focused too much on her strengths without empathizing sufficiently with her suffering. I had admitted to her that this was a fault of mine, and I'd tried hard to show more empathy. But I could not completely share her view of herself as weak and incapable of getting along in the world. She was physically strong, intelligent, and accomplished. And I had trouble ignoring the resolute strength with which she defended her weakness.

I was happy to hear from her. I looked forward to re-establishing our working relationship and the chance of making good on where I had failed her in the past. I was touched that she trusted me sufficiently to work on our earlier disagreement.

The following week, she showed up for the session. I expected at least an initial friendly greeting, but she arrived looking like a walking storm cloud. She brushed aside my attempts at cordiality and immediately got down to the business at hand. She sat hunched in her chair and began to lambaste me for having been insensitive, uncaring, and downright dangerous to her personal development.

At first I was simply shocked. I hadn't realized the degree to which she blamed me for her difficulties. But then I remembered my role as therapist and my obligation to listen carefully to my client's experience, putting aside my personal reactions for later.

But I had trouble listening. I felt wounded, misunderstood. She was unrelenting. She strung one accusation on another till they grew to a full-scale attack. I began to wonder why, if she only came to attack me, she had asked for a private session. She could have phoned me and voiced her grievances. Why pay me for a session if she only meant to read me the riot act?

Pay? Why, she saw this as a chance to redress old injuries. Surely, she said, I had once again misunderstood her. She hadn't asked for a therapeutic session, just a chance to say what was on her mind.

Now, on top of my hurt, I was also furious. I knew that I had done my best to listen patiently to her and that I could not possibly be responsible for all the blame she was heaping on me. I felt she had misused my good will to avenge an ancient grievance. But I felt that exploding at her would not solve anything. It occurred to me that her fight was not with me personally, but with inner opponents and ghosts that were too powerful for her to face alone. She was looking for satisfaction where the light shined, not where the problem was.

She felt free to attack me because I was safe! She knew that as a therapist, I was not free to simply counter-attack. I guessed that whatever ghosts she was fighting were not nearly as humane or tolerant as I was being toward her.

By attempting to understand her end of the conflict, I became detached enough to also notice how I was feeling, independently of her. The first thing I noticed was my heart beating very fast and I was feeling dizzy and disoriented. I got worried – was I about to collapse? I decided to pay attention to my body, in addition to her. Although I didn't really think I was in danger of a serious collapse, I took my fantasy seriously. Perhaps continuing to absorb her criticism was not good for my health.

So I said to her, "I notice that I feel like I'm about to faint. I'm a little worried. I like you, I think you're a great woman, but I'm not willing to die for you today." She became very still and sat there with her mouth open slightly, looking bemused. After a few moments, she said, "I didn't realize I was that important to you, that I could affect you so strongly." And then I felt myself relax. I realized we had gotten to the core of the problem. She saw me as an all-powerful but uncaring authority figure who hardly acknowledged her existence. The only way, in her mind, she could get through to me was by seeing me react clearly and powerfully.

I remembered this feeling myself when, as a child, I sometimes had to play nasty tricks on my father before he would take me seriously. It was not an ideal way to relate to him, but at least I felt that he saw me fully in those moments. But his angry reactions were not satisfying. I wanted love and acknowledgment, not anger. And because

I got some reaction, but not a satisfying reaction, provoking him became mildly addictive.

It seemed that my accuser was motivated by a similar pattern. She needed to provoke me in order to feel seen and heard by someone with as much power and authority as she projected on me. If I had simply reacted out of the anger I felt, I would have only fed her addiction. She would have seen me as one more authority figure who put her down instead of taking her seriously.

By focusing on my body experience, I was able to show her clearly, but without anger, that she had a profound effect on me, and that the effect was not pleasant. This evidently helped her reflect on what she was doing, rather than simply provoking another round of accusations. If I had merely gotten angry, it would have encouraged her to try even harder. We both would have gotten caught in a cycle of escalation that would leave both of us hurt and resentful. I cannot say that after this encounter that we parted friends. But neither were we enemies.

A week later, she called to thank me and to ask if I would be willing to resume our therapeutic work together. And work we did, cautiously at first, but later with a growing sense of trust and mutual respect.

Our initial conflict was the beginning of our relationship, not its end. Once we took the plunge, it led us on a crooked, painful path. But both of us benefited from the effort. Each came away a little wiser, with a little more appreciation both for the other and for his or her own inner strength. We proved, in the end, worthy opponents, each capable of enlightening and being enlightened by the other.

BOTTOM LINES AGAIN: BEFRIENDING CONFLICT DEEPENS RELATIONSHIPS

We've seen how the tools we developed to prepare for conflict also are useful for engaging in productive conflict. This brief introduction focuses mainly on accusations and attacks because they are an important part of nearly all conflicts.

But the field of conflict management is far broader than just dealing with accusations. Conflict is present in nearly all areas of human activity. My hope is that by befriending conflict, we can use the things that drive us apart as opportunities for personal and social growth.

When we began our exploration, I asked you to take it on faith that conflict, if we could only befriend it, could bring us riches far beyond winning our immediate interests. We have seen how time and time again, getting beneath the choppy surface of conflict reveals new, unimagined, and rewarding depths to our relationships. Conflict is, in a very strong sense, the ground of relationship itself. Relationships that grow out of well-conducted conflict are like the grapes that grow on stony, mineral-laden earth. They produce wines full of character and complexity that age well, improving rather than deteriorating with the years

1. Compare this trivial example with Steven Pinker's comments on the question of whether the collapse of the World Trade Center towers was a single incident or two incidents, in the opening chapter of his book, *The Stuff of Thought.* In that case, insurance payments of some 3.5 billion dollars rode on the "truth."

2. This method of admitting to the part of an accusation that is true, in the interest of favoring relationship over power, comes from the teachings of Arnold Mindell.